DISCOVER HER ART

Women Artists and Their Masterpieces

JEAN LEIBOWITZ & LISA LABANCA ROGERS

CHICAGO
REVIEW
PRESS

Published by Chicago Review Press Incorporated
814 North Franklin Street
Chicago, Illinois 60610
ISBN 978-1-64160-614-1

Library of Congress Control Number: 2021949576

Cover design: Sadie Teper
Cover photographs: (clockwise from upper left) Pan Yuliang, *Nude* (a.k.a. *Seated Nude*), 1953, Musée Cernuschi, Paris, France (inv. 38967-6), *droits réservés*, photo © RMN-Grand Palais / Art Resource, NY; Loïs Mailou Jones, *Self Portrait*, 1940, Smithsonian American Art Museum, Washington, DC / Art Resource, NY; Paula Modersohn-Becker, *Still Life with Goldfish Bowl*, 1906, HIP / Art Resource, NY; Mary Cassatt, *The Child's Bath*, 1893, The Art Institute of Chicago / Art Resource, NY; Maria Leontina, *Natureza Morta*, 1952, Ministry of Tourism authorization number 06/2021, National Museum of Fine Arts Collection / Brazilian Institute of Museums, copyright © Alexandre Franco Dacosta, photo by Jaime Acioli / Museu Nacional de Belas Artes; Lluïsa Vidal Puig, *Self-Portrait*, circa 1899, Museu Nacional d'Art de Catalunya, donated by Francesca Vidal and other brothers of the artist, 1935, © Museu Nacional d'Art de Catalunya, Barcelona, 2022.
Interior design: PerfecType, Nashville, TN

Printed in the United States of America
5 4 3 2

For my parents, who encouraged exploration —JL

For my mother and daughter: art makers,
art appreciators, and exceptional women —LR

Contents

Part II:
Modern Painting

Activities

Introduction

In *Discover Her Art,* you'll meet 24 professional women artists and explore their incredible paintings, which range from painstakingly realistic to wildly abstract. You'll learn about these artists' painting techniques and their challenges and successes.

Artists like Rosa Bonheur of France, Alma Woodsey Thomas of the United States, and Amrita Sher-Gil of India were recognized by their peers, were accepted into juried exhibitions, and received major awards. Rosa Bonheur was so popular that a doll was crafted in her likeness. President and Mrs. Obama chose a painting by Alma Woodsey Thomas to hang in the White House. Amrita Sher-Gil's paintings have been officially named national treasures by the government of India.

Yet few people can name more than a handful of women artists or recognize their work. That's because many museum collections and art history books do not include much art by women.

In this book, you'll get a close look at women artists from the 16th to the 20th centuries. You'll explore their works, both abstract and realistic, including landscapes, figures, portraits, and still lifes. You'll study the artists' techniques for using color, composition, perspective, and more. Then, you can try out their techniques—and create masterpieces of your own!

Getting Started

You'll get more out of *Discover Her Art* with a few supplies:

- Pencil and eraser
- Ruler
- Tracing paper

Having these supplies handy will help you follow the suggestions for learning about composition. In many chapters, you will be looking for *midpoints*, *thirds*, and *diagonals* to help understand how the artist composed the painting (see examples in the next section), and tracing paper will help you find them without marking up the artwork.

Art Vocabulary

Representational and Abstract

Representational art shows people, places, and things you can easily recognize.

Abstract art uses colors, lines, and shapes to express ideas and images. This type of art can include objects you recognize, but they are not presented in a realistic way.

Composition

Composition is how an artist arranges shapes, light and dark areas, and color to build interest and focus. Artists often use landmarks on the canvas like midpoints, thirds, and diagonals as guideposts for what to put where.

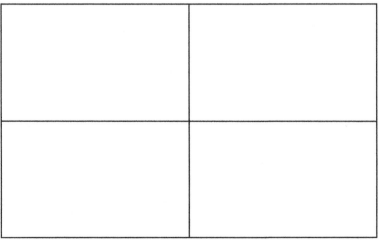

Midpoints

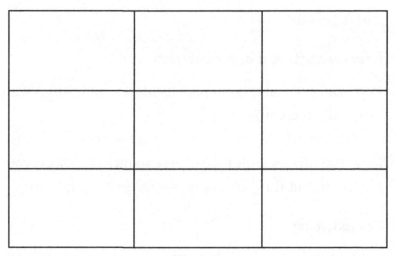

Thirds

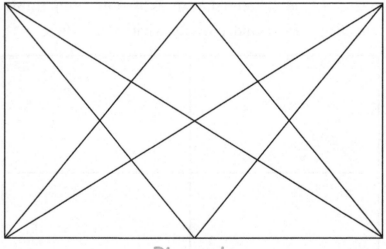

Diagonals

Color

Color makes forms look three-dimensional and lifelike and adds beauty and mood. It has four key characteristics:

- *Hue:* The name of a color, like blue or yellow.
- *Chroma:* Brightness or intensity. Fire-engine red has high chroma; brick red does not.
- *Value:* How light or dark a color is. Lavender has a lighter value than deep purple.
- *Temperature:* How cool or warm a color is. Cool colors like blue seem far away in a painting, while warm colors like red seem to come forward.

In oil painting, two ways artists can build up color are called *indirect* and *direct* painting:

- *Indirect painting:* The artist first paints the whole picture in shades of one color, often gray, like a black-and-white photo. After this underpainting, also called a *grisaille* (greez-EYE), has dried, the artist paints thin layers, or *glazes*, of color on top of it. Indirect painting is an old method that is still in use, especially for realistic art.
- *Direct painting:* The artist skips the grisaille and works in color from the beginning. Paint strokes may be thick. Direct painting is suited to modern styles and to outdoor painting where there's no time for a detailed underpainting.

Form and Shape

Forms are the three-dimensional objects in a work of art, like a tree, a person, or a piece of fruit. In a painting, the forms are two-dimensional (flat) representations of those objects; skilled drawing, use of color, and use of value make them look three-dimensional.

Shapes are flat areas in the work defined by light, color, or line.

A *positive shape* is the object you draw.

A *negative shape* is the shape of the space around a drawn object. Artists strive to create negative shapes that enhance their composition.

Perspective

Perspective creates the illusion of depth in a two-dimensional work.

Linear perspective is based on the way parallel lines get closer together with distance until they meet at a *vanishing point*. Think of a long road edged by trees. To represent this in two dimensions, an artist paints the road getting narrower and the trees getting smaller as they get farther away.

Aerial or *atmospheric perspective* is based on how colors and objects in a landscape fade with distance. Close-up forms appear crisp and colorful, while distant forms appear cooler, paler, and less distinct.

Value

Value is not just a characteristic of an individual color. It also refers to how light or dark a shape is, regardless of whether it is painted in color or black and white. Lights and darks are an important part of a painting's composition; they add emphasis, mood, and feeling, and make forms look three-dimensional.

A value scale (appendix, p. 175) helps painters identify lights and darks. Darker colors will be closer to black on the value scale, while lighter colors will be closer to white.

One way artists use value scales is when they paint a grisaille. Imagine a red apple on a table near a window. The apple is light on the side facing the window. The other side is dark. For her grisaille, the artist chooses pale and middle grays for the side facing the window. She adds white for highlights. She uses a very dark gray for the unlit side. When the underpainting has dried, she paints over it with pinks, bright reds, and dark reds that match each of the values in the grisaille.

PART I

Classical Painting and Other Realistic Styles

Classical techniques, developed long ago by European artists, include formal compositions, indirect painting, and smooth paint surfaces that create illusions of depth and volume. Classical art training was long and rigorous. Students learned to handle chalk, charcoal, pencils, and paints. They learned to draw and paint objects, drapery, landscapes, and live models through long practice and by copying masterpieces. After years of practice, they became accomplished painters.

In the late 1800s, innovative European artists grew restless with traditional art. They experimented with new ways to paint, developing Impressionist and Post-Impressionist styles. Their compositions and subjects, though still representational, became less formal, and they used lighter, brighter colors and looser, more obvious brushstrokes.

Lavinia Fontana, *Portrait of a Lady with a Dog,*
1590s. Oil on panel, 38¼ × 28½ in. (97.1 × 72.4 cm).
Mackelvie Trust Collection, Auckland Art Gallery
Toi o Tāmaki, New Zealand, purchased 1956. Photo
credit: Auckland Art Gallery Toi o Tāmaki.

CHAPTER 1

Lavinia Fontana

Arrive

Welcome! We're starting with a portrait painted in Italy more than 400 years ago. Long before photographs, a portrait was the only way to preserve someone's image. Because artists needed to make their paying patrons happy, the resulting portrait often idealized the subject's appearance, flattered their character, and highlighted their position in society. *Portrait of a Lady with a Dog* is a perfect example of all three.

Explore

Although the head is the focal point, the painting's abundant small details really draw our attention. They communicate key details about this woman's life. The lace, pearls, and gold embroidery are evidence of her wealth, and the dog was a popular symbol of marriage and faithfulness. Symbolism aside, let's look at what makes this early portrait a great lesson in painting.

- What makes this a classical portrait pose?
- What does it mean to work from big to small?
- How did Fontana liven up the color scheme?

Composition

In this portrait Fontana uses a simple, classical composition that portrait artists use to this day. The seated figure takes up most of the canvas and is shown from the lap up. The body angles slightly left while the woman faces us in three-quarter view. This gives us a sense of the roundness of her head by showing us her features and the shaded side of her face.

Painting Strategy

The artist painted in the realistic tradition of her day. The portrait is highly accurate though not very expressive; for example, the face gives us little sense of the sitter's personality, but the exquisite details tell us a lot about her position in society. Examine the way Fontana perfectly captures the lacy cuffs and collar, the pearls, and the embroidery. The dog deserves a close look, too, to appreciate how carefully Fontana rendered its form and expression.

To make this portrait, the artist would have worked *from big to small*, starting with larger brushes to make the main shapes. Then she would have added surface detail with smaller and smaller brushes, ending perhaps with painting the lacy threads. The result is that every mark is exquisitely sharp, giving the painting a crisp, tight feeling.

Light

Portrait artists pay close attention to lighting to avoid casting unflattering shadows. The glow on the forehead shows that Fontana used soft lighting, perhaps from a high window, angled slightly from above. Artists still use soft, angled portrait lighting, because it showcases the eyes, gives volume to the face, and avoids harsh shadows.

Color

Brown is the dominant color, but because it shows up in different ways, the painting doesn't feel dull or monochromatic. See if you can identify browns that have different values (dark to pale), hues (deep brown to gold), and temperatures (cool to warm).

The woman's face stands out because of the contrasts of value, hue, and temperature between its warm pink hues and the deep brown behind it.

Adding It Up

This portrait of a wealthy married woman is classical and formal. Portraits today have a lot in common with this one, especially the position of the figure and the lighting. The exquisite detail, however, is typical of Fontana's day and demonstrates the patience required to complete a piece in this style.

About Lavinia Fontana

Born in Bologna, Italy, in 1552, Lavinia Fontana was one of the first European women painters to have a successful artistic career, and she was highly regarded for her expertise.

Her portraits were admired for their precise renderings of lace and embroidery, as well as how they captured family dynamics. Besides her ability to paint with remarkable accuracy, Fontana's portraits of her subjects, one of whom was Pope Paul V, made her a sought-after artist. Fontana created elaborate altarpieces for churches and large mythological scenes, all unusual projects for a woman of her time. "This excellent Painter, to say the truth, in every way prevails above the condition of her sex and is a most remarkable person," said one patron. The groundbreaking artist Sofonisba Anguissola (1532–1625), who had been taught by Michelangelo and was a court painter to King Philip II of Spain, was another patron.

Fontana was educated, earning a doctor of letters degree in 1580. Though elite women studied academic subjects at the University of Bologna, they could not attend the city's art academy, because of restrictions on women working with nude models.

Like many of the painters featured in this book, Fontana benefited from her place in an artistic family. Her father, Prospero Fontana, was a successful fresco painter in Bologna who encouraged his daughter's creativity and trained her in artistic techniques. Her mother came from a Bolognese family of publishers and printmakers. In a reverse of traditional roles, Fontana's husband, also an artist, served as her assistant. Acknowledging her earnings potential, her marriage agreement specified that future income from her artworks would substitute for the traditional dowry paid by the bride's family to the groom's. Her father's business, which it was expected she would inherit and run, was another source of potential income. Besides her painting career, Fontana was a mother who had 11 children.

Despite all of her obligations, her reputation surpassed that of her father, and she created at least 100 works. Her last known painting is a nude figural representation of the Roman goddess Minerva. She died in Rome in 1614.

In 1598, poet Giulio Cesare Croce wrote of Fontana, "In painting there are those who know the great wonder of nature, Lavinia Fontana, noble painter, unique in the world like a phoenix."

Ten Ways to Build Your Art Skills

Throughout *Discover Her Art*, you'll find activities that will help you build drawing and painting skills. They let you practice techniques used by the artists in the paintings you'll explore. If you do these activities over and over again, you will develop art habits that will continually strengthen your artwork.

On your first few times through these activities, follow the instructions using drawing supplies. When you feel ready, repeat them using your favorite painting supplies. Keep your work so you can see your progress!

You'll Need

Pencils and an eraser
Tracing paper
Ruler
Sketchbook or blank paper
Colored pencils, crayons, or markers
Favorite painting supplies

Artemisia Gentileschi, *Esther Before Ahasuerus,*
circa 1630. Oil on canvas, 82 × 107¾ in.
(208.3 × 273.7 cm). The Metropolitan Museum of
Art, New York, gift of Elinor Dorrance Ingersoll,
1969 (69.281). Image copyright © The Metropolitan
Museum of Art. Image source: Art Resource, NY.

CHAPTER 2

Artemisia Gentileschi

Arrive

Arriving before the monumental *Esther Before Ahasuerus* is like arriving in the middle of a play. Queen Esther, clothed in gold, swoons before the king. This is a symbolic moment in Jewish history. Persian king Ahasuerus has agreed to a plan to murder all the Jews in the kingdom, not knowing that Esther, his own wife, is Jewish. Though challenging her husband is forbidden, Esther decides to try. She is quickly overcome with fear and faints into her servants' arms. The king leans toward her. Is he sympathetic—or angry? What happens next?

Explore

Let's take a closer look at the classical design strategy in *Esther Before Ahasuerus*. Using key points on the canvas's edges, the artist created a geometric framework for this painting, a common practice in this era. Here are three questions we'll explore:

- Where is the line that's the key to the design?
- What other lines guide the design?
- Why are the figures in such unnatural positions?

Composition

Let's look at the stage Gentileschi created. In the foreground, a little left of center, is a line between the floor tiles. Follow that line from the front of the bottom stair to the top of the column in the dark background. That line is an *axis* that organizes the whole painting. The top of it functions as the *vanishing point* for linear perspective. Look for the lines that lead to it—for example, between the floor tiles, on the wall behind the throne, and on the stair at bottom right.

The axis line also splits the painting, squeezing Esther into the smaller area on the left. Within that space, the vanishing point even shapes the women's postures. Notice how you can draw straight lines from the vanishing point that follow the tops of the women's heads and go across Esther's shoulders and waist. Some of Esther's dress folds even lead to the vanishing point.

Other hidden lines guide this composition. Trace or imagine a diagonal from top left to bottom right. In what way does Esther's figure follow it? Now look at the bottom of the axis line. What parts of Esther and Ahasuerus point to it?

Lights and Darks

Light tells us exactly what to focus on in this painting. As if in a theater, Esther is lit sharply from above. This painting is clearly about Esther's dramatic moment and not about the king's response.

Color

Artemisia dressed her characters in fabrics and colors of royalty: sumptuous velvet and silk in gold, blue, and purple. Esther's golden gown stands out from the dark and cool colors in the rest of the painting, enhancing her star quality.

Adding It Up

Gentileschi designed *Esther Before Ahasuerus* as if she were directing actors on a stage. Her classical composition framework, dramatic lighting, and brilliant colors cause Esther, the star, to shine even as she falls. This is Esther's moment, her story.

About Artemisia Gentileschi

Artemisia Gentileschi learned to draw at an early age and painted masterpieces in her teens, but she could not read or write until she was in her 20s.

Born in 1593, she grew up in Rome. Like other prominent women artists, she trained with her father, who created grand, formal figure paintings and frescoes in sumptuous colors. Orazio Gentileschi's work was influenced by the dramatic lighting effects of Caravaggio, and so was his daughter's. She incorporated Caravaggio's theatricality and immediacy into her painting.

Her formal training began at about age 15, and her first dated work, *Susanna and the Elders*, was completed two years later, in 1610. Her superb skills meant that she was able to build a successful career, with her paintings acquired in her lifetime by private collectors.

Most of her surviving works represent allegorical or biblical figures. She also painted portraits, including the remarkable *Self-Portrait as the Allegory of Painting*, in which she works, intent at the easel, as if she were the spirit of painting itself.

She suffered crises in her personal life. After she was assaulted at age 18 by an artist hired to teach her drawing and perspective, she testified at his trial, which lasted five months. The day after her attacker was convicted and sentenced to exile, she married. She and her husband left Rome for Florence. In Florence, she created a new life, setting up her own studio and teaching other women painters. She also gave birth to four children. Artemisia Gentileschi was internationally known, and her paintings were sought after. She was the first woman accepted into Florence's acclaimed Accademia delle Arti del Disegno. Invited to join her father in England, where he was painter to the court of Charles I, she helped him create nine canvases for the ceiling of a royal country house. King Philip IV of Spain commissioned her to paint the mythological *Hercules and Omphale*.

Gentileschi had great confidence in her abilities. In a 1649 letter to the Sicilian collector Don Antonio Ruffo, she wrote, "A woman's name raises doubts until her work is seen." Later that same year, she boldly stated, "I will show Your Most Illustrious Lordship what a woman can do."

"The works will speak for themselves," she declared.

In 1651 Gentileschi wrote to Don Ruffo that she was recovering from an illness and would finish several works in progress by the spring. She is believed to have died in 1652 or 1653.

Rachel Ruysch, *Still Life with Flowers on a Marble Tabletop*, 1716. Oil on canvas, 19 × 15½ in. (48.5 × 39.5 cm). Rijksmuseum, Amsterdam, purchased with the support of the Vereniging Rembrandt. Photo credit: Rijksmuseum, Amsterdam.

CHAPTER 3

Rachel Ruysch

Arrive

These flowers burst out of their vase with such vitality you can almost smell them. They are lively, beautiful, and mysterious. And since this painting has much to say about classical techniques, it's worth spending time getting to know it. Let's take a deeper look.

Explore

Rachel Ruysch was a successful painter. Her *Still Life with Flowers on a Marble Tabletop* is from the Dutch Golden Age of still life, when artists painted familiar objects in complicated arrangements. Many, like this one, have hidden details. Explore and see what you find; when you're done, look at the whole painting again.

- How did Ruysch elevate this painting from a simple flower arrangement to one that's like fireworks?
- How did she paint so accurately?

Composition and Design

While flowers are a common subject of paintings, Ruysch made them unexpectedly dramatic. Where does most of the drama come from? Is it composition, color, or light?

Let's start with composition. The bouquet almost fills the canvas. The flowers bloom along a diagonal, which adds movement and depth: the flowers are closer to us at the lower left than at the upper right. The flowers' fullness and the strong diagonal certainly add some drama to the painting—yet they're not the main source of drama.

What about color? Ruysch's pale, warm colors stand out brilliantly against the dull background. Look carefully at the small shifts in color within each flower and even within each petal. These shifts required exceptional skill in observation, color mixing, and brushwork. The colors definitely add drama, but they're not the primary source either.

Finally, let's talk about the light. The flowers stand out brilliantly against the dark background and tabletop. This strong value contrast is what really drives the drama. In a bouquet of flowers, this simple idea—lighting a small area and leaving the rest dark—is both unexpected and beautiful. It turns the flowers into fireworks and takes them from ordinary to extraordinary.

Painting into the Details

Sketching and painting an arrangement like this could take weeks or months. Classical artists often painted using thin coats of oil paints called *glazes*, which built up rich colors and smooth surfaces. Sometimes artists glazed on top of a grisaille underpainting. Every glazing layer needed to dry before adding the next one, and because oil paints dry slowly, the process took a long time. Tiny details like the bugs would be added at the very end.

So how might Ruysch have painted these flowers before they wilted? She didn't! To get around this problem, she probably made many sketches while the flowers were fresh. She might have first painted the basic shapes and values, keeping it simple. As flowers faded, she could add new ones to her bouquet and could use her early sketches for guidance. She likely turned to botanical drawings for further reference. Her father, after all, was a noted botanist, and she could have used drawings by him.

Adding It Up

Ruysch took her bouquet of flowers and made them into a dramatic masterpiece. The lighting drives the drama, boosted by a dynamic composition and warm, lively color. This astonishing image draws viewers in to look for secret details.

About Rachel Ruysch

Early still life paintings with flowers usually included other objects: silver pitchers, bowls of fruit, and hunks of cheese, sometimes backed by views of landscapes. Born in 1664, Rachel Ruysch was one of the earliest painters to specialize in still lifes that centered on flowers themselves, in all of their beauty, variety, and detail.

She came from an intellectual family. Her mother's father was an architect, and her father was a highly regarded anatomy and botany professor who also painted. After she showed promise in drawing, Ruysch trained at age 15 with a highly skilled painter of still lifes and florals, Willem van Aelst, who had been court painter to Italy's Medici family. He innovated by composing his floral designs in a natural-looking way, rather than the more typical stiff, *symmetrical* arrangements, where the left and right sides of the painting are mirror images of one another. Ruysch might have been inspired by him to do the same. She also studied with Maria Sibylla Merian, noted for her groundbreaking work in entomology—the study of insects—and her accurate representations of bugs and flowers. Ruysch meticulously crafted her paintings. Her flowers seem to be botanically correct, but she went further, vividly infusing them with naturalness. She planned her bouquets around color and shape. Her time-consuming approach limited her to two or three works each year.

Ruysch's skill earned her acclaim, including membership in The Hague's Painters Guild and selection as a court painter to the elector palatine of Bavaria. Her paintings sold at high prices to an international set of collectors. She married a Dutch portrait painter, had 10 children, and continued painting into her eighties. She died in 1750.

Adélaïde Labille-Guiard, *Self-Portrait with Two Pupils, Mademoiselle Marie Gabrielle Capet (1761–1818) and Mademoiselle Carreaux de Rosemond (Died 1788)*, 1785. Oil on canvas, 83 × 59½ in. (210.8 × 151.1 cm). The Metropolitan Museum of Art, New York, gift of Julia A. Berwind, 1953 (53.225.5). Image copyright © The Metropolitan Museum of Art. Image source: Art Resource, NY.

CHAPTER 4

Adélaïde Labille-Guiard

Arrive

Imagine you've arrived at the Paris Salon of 1785. It's the greatest art event and competition of the year. Paintings fill the grand galleries from floor to ceiling. In the crowded rooms it is difficult to decide what to look at. Suddenly, this painting by Adélaïde Labille-Guiard grabs your attention. At five feet wide by seven feet high, this enormous self-portrait with two of the artist's favorite pupils earned a prime spot on the wall. The painting is a bold declaration that Labille-Guiard has earned her place in a field, and a salon, crowded with men.

Explore

This painting creates immediate impact while drawing you in to delight in the details. Let's explore:

- What elements of design, light, and color help you appreciate the painting right away?
- What are the more subtle elements of brushwork and detail?

Composition

You probably realized right away that the artist is the focus of the painting. Several design elements direct your eye to her. First, her face is right in the middle. But notice, too, how the easel's edge and the figures of the students form a "V" pattern that draws your eye to her face, paintbrush, palette, and knees.

Lights and Darks

A strong value contrast also emphasizes that the artist is the main subject. Labille-Guiard set up the light source so that it lit up her own figure but barely brushed the cheeks of her pupils and left the rest of the setting dark.

Color

The painting features a full spectrum of color: red, orange, yellow, green, and blue. The most important single color is the billowy ocean of the artist's cool, gray-blue silk dress. It owes its impact to contrasts; it is lighter, cooler, and brighter than the deep tones around it.

Getting into the Details

Composition, color, and light are important, but a classical artist also had to draw well, since paintings began with sketching the composition on the canvas. Labille-Guiard showed off her drawing skills here by rendering faces from three different angles and accurately capturing details of the setting. She also had to know how to mix colors and apply paint to create smooth surfaces and realistic forms. She showed her painting skills by creating varied, believable surfaces, including wood, cloth, and skin. The pupil's hand on the chair and the ruffle on her sleeve are perfect examples of combining great drawing with superb painting. You may wonder why Labille-Guiard was painting in a ball gown; the likely reason was to prove to potential portrait clients that she could make their own gowns look just as exquisite.

Adding It Up

Labille-Guiard's self-portrait shows how a great painting can work both from a distance and close up. It demonstrates mastery in composition, portraiture, drapery, detail, light, and color. It also works as an advertisement. If you went to the 1785 Salon in search of a portrait artist, this painting might convince you whom to hire.

About Adélaïde Labille-Guiard

Like other women artists of her time whose creative opportunities were held back by society's expectations, Adélaïde Labille-Guiard, born in Paris in 1749, began by painting miniature portraits. As her career flourished, neither she nor her artistic subjects would remain small or overlooked. *Self-Portrait with Two Pupils* is nearly life-size in its celebration of women artists as it declares their place in the art world.

Labille-Guiard benefited from growing up in art-centric Paris and living near the world-famous art museum the Louvre, but she did not come from a family of artists. She must have shown early promise, though, because her father allowed her to study with an artist who specialized in miniatures.

Marriage at age 20 did not limit Labille-Guiard's ambition or her ability to study her craft: she listed her profession as *artist* on her marriage certificate. The same year, she joined an artists' guild, the Académie de Saint-Luc, which gave women artists the opportunity to show their work.

She was tutored in using pigmented chalk-like crayons, called *pastels*, by renowned pastel artist Maurice Quentin de La Tour, exhibited a miniature and a pastel in 1774 at the Académie de Saint-Luc, and studied oil painting with a prize-winning portrait artist. She opened her own studio and taught other women painters. The two pupils portrayed in the self-portrait were her favorites.

In 1783, Labille-Guiard and painter Élisabeth Vigée Le Brun were admitted on the same day to the prestigious Académie Royale de Peinture et de Sculpture, based at the Louvre. Entry to the academy required a recommendation from a member and election by other members. With two women already studying at the Académie Royale, the admission of Labille-Guiard and Vigée Le Brun led the academy to immediately impose a limit of four women members.

Labille-Guiard challenged that quota, arguing against it in a 1790 speech. Her position won by a majority vote, but the Académie Royale soon closed, and when it reopened, under a different name and management, it no longer accepted women members.

Labille-Guiard received valuable commissions and exhibited regularly in the Paris Salon. She showed at least 14 portraits in its 1791 exhibition, in which 20 women were among the 255 participating artists.

Though she received commissions from the monarchy of France, she supported the French Revolution against them and even painted the portrait of leading insurrectionist Maximilien Robespierre. Yet in 1793 revolutionaries destroyed a half-finished painting of King Louis XVI's brother that she had hoped would be her greatest achievement.

Adélaïde Labille-Guiard died at her French country home in 1803.

Activity 1: Copy a Masterpiece

Copying paintings is great practice and is an important part of classical art training. No doubt Adélaïde Labille-Guiard would have copied a lot of paintings during her studies. You can copy art from books and websites or when you visit museums.

You'll Need

Pencils and an eraser
Tracing paper
Ruler
Sketchbook or paper
Favorite painting supplies

1. Start with a painting in this book. First, get a feel for the painting by tracing it. Measure the length of each side.
2. To copy it, work in your sketchbook—not from your tracing. Draw a rectangle with the same proportions as its image in this book (for example, the same size or twice as big). It's helpful to lightly mark the thirds, as well as the *quarters* (one-fourth, one-half, and three-fourths) along the edges.
3. Copy the big shapes in the painting first, being careful to get their size and placement right. Make your first lines light so you can erase mistakes, then darken your lines when you're sure they're correct.
4. Shade in the darkest values. Then shade the middle values, making them halfway between the dark values and the white of the paper.
5. Stop here or add more detail. Copy paintings as often as you can. Notice what you learn each time. And try it in paint when you feel ready. You could draw it first and then fill it in using different values of gray.

Rosa Bonheur, *The Horse Fair*, 1853–1855. Oil on canvas, 96¼ × 199½ in. (244.5 × 506.7 cm). The Metropolitan Museum of Art, New York, gift of Cornelius Vanderbilt, 1887 (87.25). Image copyright © The Metropolitan Museum of Art. Image source: Art Resource, NY.

CHAPTER 5

Rosa Bonheur

Arrive

If you needed to upgrade your transportation in the mid-1800s, you would go to a horse fair, like this one near Paris. In this enormous, energetic painting, horses circle left to right under a stormy sky. Sun breaks through to light up the focal point. Something has startled two of the horses.

Look at the painting's format. With its long shape and right-facing movement, the painting encourages us to read it like a story, from left to right. And what a story: in real life, the painting is as long as a pickup truck. Imagine the drama you would feel standing in front of it.

Explore

The Horse Fair was painted in the 1850s in a classical style. It is detailed, realistic, and carefully designed. Let's take a closer look at the toolkit Rosa Bonheur brought to this painting.

- How did Bonheur use classical composition tools?
- How did she use value contrast?
- What color scheme did she use?

Composition

As a 19th-century realist painter, Bonheur would probably have used the geometry of her canvas to provide a simple framework to order, balance, and keep track of her design. Without that framework, it would be easy to make a mistake when working on such a huge canvas.

Let's imagine how she might have begun. Start by tracing a line across the middle of the image. Notice how Bonheur used that line to position the horses' backs and shoulders. She also used the midpoint on the left edge as her vanishing point: the slanted line of trees starts there and ends on the top edge, the trees getting bigger as they get closer to us. The trees meet the top edge at the one-quarter mark, another guidepost for her composition.

Now let's look at how Bonheur structured the main action, where the horses are rearing. Imagine or trace a vertical line down the middle of the painting. It separates the light and dark areas. It's also where Bonheur placed the head of the rearing white horse—the painting's star—to grab your attention. What about the crossed legs of the black horse? Let's see what guidelines Bonheur might have used. Imagine or trace a big X whose lines cross where the legs cross. One side of it should run parallel to the horse's belly and meet the treetops at that point one-quarter of the way in from the right edge. Now trace the other side of this X, noticing that it follows a break in the clouds—in fact, the cloud break is angled to direct our eyes to the main action.

Lights and Darks

Bonheur placed the greatest value contrasts, between light and dark, in the middle to draw your eye there. If all of the horses were brown and black, you would not have the strong focal point created by sunlight on the white horses.

Colors

Most of *The Horse Fair*'s colors form what's called an *analogous* color scheme—the chosen colors are close together on a color wheel. (See the color wheel in the appendix, p. 76.) The blue-gray skies, blue-green jackets, gold-green trees, and golden earth unify the huge picture.

Adding It Up

The Horse Fair's strong yet simple design strategy and its unifying color scheme create a tight composition across its great size, while the sharp value contrasts highlight the central action.

About Rosa Bonheur

"I wed art. It is my husband, my world, my life's dream, the air I breathe," Rosa Bonheur said. "I know nothing else, feel nothing else, think nothing else. My soul finds in it the most complete satisfaction."

Born in the French countryside in 1822, Bonheur practiced the alphabet by drawing animals beginning with each letter. Bonheur's father taught drawing, her mother was one of his students, and all four Bonheur children became artists. The family moved to Paris when she was six. She did not study at the academies; instead she was taught by her father and learned by copying works at the Louvre. For Bonheur, art was essential. To do her best work, she felt, she had to enter a world where women didn't ordinarily go—and she got permission from the police to do so. She dressed like a man, cutting her hair and wearing pants and boots, so she could go to horse fairs and stockyards without being bothered.

She studied animal anatomy to capture the movements of the horses, dogs, and sheep that she painted and sculpted. She collected animals—a monkey, a parrot, a lion—in order to accurately paint them. She was a perfectionist.

Her paintings could be small and quiet, like *Rabbits Nibbling Carrots*. They could be bold and dramatic, like *The Horse Fair*, which took two years to complete.

Bonheur showed *The Horse Fair* to England's Queen Victoria at Buckingham Palace. It was sold three times before being bought in 1887 for $53,000 by an American, Cornelius Vanderbilt, who donated it to the Metropolitan Museum of Art in New York.

At age 24, Bonheur won a gold medal, for six paintings and two sculptures, at the Paris Salon, a rare honor for a woman. In 1865, she became the first woman to receive France's highest award, the Cross of the Legion of Honor, which Empress Eugénie, the wife of the French emperor Napoleon III, personally delivered to Bonheur at her studio.

Bonheur had long-term intimate relationships with painters Nathalie Micas and Anna Klumpke. Of Micas, with whom she had been close since she was 14 and lived with for more than 40 years, Bonheur wrote, "Had I been a man, I would have married her." After Micas's death, Bonheur asked Klumpke, who as a child had played with a doll made in Rosa's likeness, to live with her in a "divine marriage of two souls." Klumpke's portrait of Bonheur, depicted at her easel with her medal prominently displayed on her jacket, is also at the Metropolitan Museum of Art.

Rosa Bonheur died of influenza in 1899 at her country house in France.

Activity 2: Work on a Series

Rosa Bonheur focused on painting animals. She spent years perfecting these skills through practice and repetition. Now it's your turn.

You'll Need

Favorite drawing and painting supplies
Paper

1. Pick a simple subject—one to three objects. It could be anything you like to draw: fruit, a pitcher, a plant, or your pet or favorite animal. You can set up a small still life on a table, or work from photographs.
2. Make two or three drawings each week until you have completed 10.
3. Be curious, not critical. As you finish each picture, ask yourself what's great about it and what could be better.
4. Once you have 10 drawings of your subject, congratulate yourself on having finished the series. Compare your first attempt to your last. What differences do you notice? What did you learn?
5. Repeat the series practice with paint or with other subjects whenever you can.

Berthe Morisot, *View of Paris from the Trocadero*, 1871–1873. Oil on canvas, 18⅛ × 32⅛ in. (46.0 × 81.6 cm). Santa Barbara Museum of Art, gift of Mrs. Hugh N. Kirkland (1974.21.2). Photo credit: Santa Barbara Museum of Art.

Berthe Morisot

Arrive

A little girl gazes out at Paris in the early 1870s. While her mother and her aunt chat, she looks toward the heart of the city. We see what she sees: a great lawn, the Seine river, and distant buildings, the land stretching out to the horizon.

Explore

Berthe Morisot was a talented member of the Impressionist movement. Her landscape *View of Paris from the Trocadero* is a bit unusual, because she is known mainly for portrait and figure work. Women artists had less freedom than men to wander and paint outdoors, and this painting was done near the artist's home in the Trocadero Gardens. The figures are Morisot's sisters and her niece.

For this painting we'll explore one key question:

* How did Morisot create a convincing sense of distance in this medium-sized canvas?

Composition

Composition is the first tool Morisot used to create space and depth. The painting has three main layers, one behind the other. Morisot painted each layer differently. In the foreground are the figures, fence, and lawn, which hold most of our attention. The foreground takes up most of the lower half and has the largest shapes and the brightest colors. It also has the strongest contrasts—the black-and-white figures stand out against that huge curved expanse of green.

The midground lies between the far end of the lawn and the line of trees across the river. It's smaller than the foreground and though many small figures invite a closer look, they are painted without any detail. Other than the trees, the midground colors are mostly pale earth hues that let the bright green lawn pop forward.

The background, the smallest layer, shows the city and the sky. Its cool blues and grays appear far away. The little girl may be gazing at the gold dome above the horizon, painted to draw our attention into the distance as well. With the figures strongly anchoring the left third of the painting, the dome also balances the composition by pulling our attention to the right.

Scale

Morisot used scale as another tool to create a sense of distance. Size differences help us know that the women and child are close to us and at the top of a hill. Even though the green area is painted in a flat manner, we know it slopes downward because the figures at the base are so small.

Atmospheric Perspective

Atmospheric perspective is how artists emphasize distance using light and color. Outdoors, nearby forms are bright and crisp and value contrasts can be sharp. Distant forms appear bluish and less distinct. Notice how Morisot used atmospheric perspective to make the background seem far away.

Adding It Up

Morisot takes us into distant Paris through distinctive foreground, midground, and background areas. As we look farther away, contrasts become less intense, colors

CLASSICAL PAINTING AND OTHER REALISTIC STYLES

cool off, detail falls away, and figures and forms get smaller and smaller.

While the Trocadero still exists, the view is very different now. Today the little girl would be able to see the Eiffel Tower from this park!

About Berthe Morisot

Born in Bourges, France, in 1841, Berthe Morisot was the first woman member of the Impressionist group that included Claude Monet, Camille Pissarro, and Pierre-Auguste Renoir. Their works were fresh and vibrant. Their immediacy and lack of formality shocked viewers. Of the Impressionists' second exhibit in 1876, a critic from the French newspaper *Le Figaro* said the "so-called art" was created by "five or six lunatics blinded by ambition, one of them a woman."

Morisot understood that sexism affected how her work was received. "I don't think there has ever been a man who treated a woman as an equal," she wrote, "and it is all I would have asked, for I know I'm worth as much as they."

Morisot's great-uncle was Jean-Honoré Fragonard, a famous painter of lush romantic scenes, and she and her older sister Edma showed artistic talent early. Her wealthy family provided them with private instructors, and they studied paintings at the Louvre to hone their technical skills. They were influenced by realistic landscape painter Jean-Baptiste-Camille Corot, who advocated sketching outdoors as preparation for a studio painting.

The Morisot sisters shared a studio, and both showed paintings in the Paris Salon in 1864. Edma gave up painting after her marriage, but the two remained close. Berthe Morisot painted Edma in domestic scenes, including *The Cradle*, where she gazes at her infant daughter. In *View of Paris from the Trocadero*, the figures are thought to represent Edma, their sister Yves, and Yves's young daughter.

Berthe's work focused on the domestic life around her. She captured reflective indoor moments and active outdoor scenes with freshness and vitality. Her loose brushwork and brilliant light effects fill her paintings with energy and life.

Though Morisot seemed to envy Edma's domestic happiness, she remained devoted to her art. "Work is the sole purpose of my existence," she wrote in an 1871 letter to Edma.

Morisot later married Eugène Manet, the brother of the painter Édouard Manet. Eugène supported her artistic career, encouraging her and helping her hang paintings for exhibitions. Their daughter, Julie Manet, also painted, and posed for several of her mother's tender portraits.

Berthe Morisot produced more than 800 artworks, including pastels, oils, watercolors, and sketches, before she died of pneumonia in Paris in 1895.

Activity 3: Walk Away from Your Work

Artists often step away from their easels while they are painting. Walking away helps you see your work as viewers will and reveals errors you wouldn't see up close. Berthe Morisot might have stepped back over and over to make sure her foreground, midground, and background were creating an illusion of depth in her view of Paris.

You'll Need

Favorite drawing and painting supplies
Paper or sketchbook
A way to prop up your work when you walk away—if you don't have an easel, pin your paper to a bulletin board, use a clipboard, or tape it to a piece of cardboard.

1. Start a drawing.
2. Every 5 to 10 minutes as you draw, prop up your work, then turn around and walk five steps away.
3. Look at your work. Every time, ask yourself what's working and what needs to change. Notice how much easier it is to see your whole drawing from a distance compared to being up close.
4. Repeat this with a painting.
5. Remember to practice walking away from every drawing and painting you do!

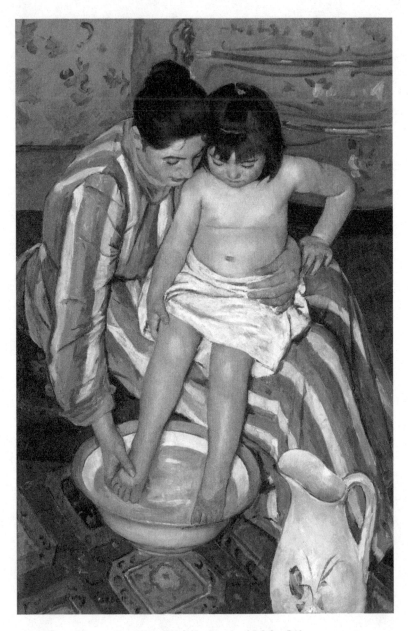

Mary Cassatt, *The Child's Bath*, 1893. Oil on canvas, 39½ × 26 in. (100.3 × 66.1 cm). The Art Institute of Chicago, Robert A. Waller Fund (1910.2). Photo credit: The Art Institute of Chicago / Art Resource, NY.

CHAPTER 7

Mary Cassatt

Arrive

Look at that solid little person settled safely on her mother's lap. She peers down at her feet wiggling in warm water. Her mother whispers in her ear. This remarkable painting captures an intimate moment in a family's day, but it also captures something much bigger: the connection between the two figures and the emotions that come with it.

Explore

Mary Cassatt, an Impressionist master, developed a representational approach that was lively and experimental, mixing loose brushwork with accurate drawing and unexpected composition strategies. She was known for painting women and their children in spontaneous moments together. In this example, we'll explore the following:

- How did Cassatt use a single shape to organize the painting?
- How do pattern, light, and color support the painting design?

Composition

Artists often build their designs inside a large shape that anchors the composition. This painting is a great example. Notice how the figures, bowl, and pitcher are contained in one continuous shape that takes up most of the canvas. It's held together by the stripes on the mother's dress, which lead our eyes down, across, and out of the painting.

Pattern, Color, and Light

Pattern, color, and light work together to focus our eyes on the child. With patterns on every surface, the canvas keeps our eyes busy. The child's body is the only area that's not patterned; it stands out because of that difference. Three distinct color themes also help her stand out. The background and foreground are full of darker and *lower chroma* colors, letting the big shape jump out with cool whites, greens, and purples in the dress, bowl, and pitcher. The child's pale, warm flesh tones form yet another color theme that stands out from its surroundings. The child is a study in contrasts while she studies her feet.

Adding It Up

Cassatt's use of a big shape and her masterful use of pattern, color, and light create a scene in which mother and child seem inseparable from each other within their own little world. Despite the title, this is not just a painting of a child's bath but also a painting about a relationship.

About Mary Cassatt

Mary Cassatt was a leader among painters in the late 1800s and early 1900s, when "modern" art began. Cassatt was born in 1844 near Philadelphia, Pennsylvania, but mostly lived and worked in Europe, especially Paris.

As a child, Cassatt spent four years in France and Germany, and European art and culture influenced her. At 16, she decided to become an artist, despite her family's objections.

Cassatt enrolled at the Pennsylvania Academy of the Fine Arts but found her classes dull. She convinced her parents to let her study in Paris. Even then, independent Cassatt set her own course, devoting a year in Italy to learn from its masterpieces. Her first solo show was in 1891 at Paris's Durand-Ruel gallery.

Cassatt was the only American invited to join the group of artists best known as the Impressionists, though she and her close friend Edgar Degas, who invited her, preferred to call them "Independents." After viewing an 1890 exhibit of Japanese woodblock prints at the École des Beaux-Arts, Cassatt was inspired to create delicate etchings. In a melding of two artistic styles, she featured women in intimate moments, such as bathing or brushing their hair. Upon viewing one of her Japanese-inspired prints, Degas said, "I am not willing to admit that a woman can draw that well." He bought that picture.

Cassatt did not marry or have children, but her parents and sister, and then her brother and his family, joined her in Paris. She pursued her career as an artist, ran the household, and cared for her family. They inspired her and often became the subjects of her paintings.

Mary Cassatt wasn't the only person to paint women and children, but she changed how they appear in paintings. Classical paintings mostly showed women and children as beautiful, helpless, or innocent. Cassatt painted women who look ordinary, with strong character, in charge of their actions.

For any painter, sharp eyesight is crucial, and the loss of it devastating. After Mary Cassatt's eyesight began to blur, she was diagnosed with cataracts, in which the eye's lens becomes opaque. She was forced to give up painting at age 70 and died in France in 1926 at age 82.

Cecilia Beaux, *Dorothea and Francesca*, 1898. Oil on
canvas, 80⅛ × 46 in. (203.5 × 116.8 cm), signed, lower
left: "Cecilia Beaux." The Art Institute of Chicago,
A. A. Munger Collection (1921.109). Photo credit:
The Art Institute of Chicago / Art Resource, NY.

CHAPTER 8

Cecilia Beaux

Arrive

When you arrive at this painting you've actually entered a barn! That is where Cecilia Beaux's two young friends practiced their dancing. The two figures glide forward into the light. Young Francesca concentrates as she shows off a new step, and she and Dorothea admire her gracefully pointed foot.

Explore

This life-size figure painting is tightly framed within a narrow rectangular format. The painting captures a brief moment in a dance step, making it seem spontaneous and casual, like a snapshot. In fact, the design is not spontaneous at all. Let's explore:

- How did Cecilia Beaux create balance and movement?
- In what ways did she use classical composition methods?
- How do light and color influence the mood?

Composition

Beaux wanted her figures to look like they were moving, but her models could not have held this pose for long. So although Beaux might have sketched from life for practice, the painting is not faithful to a specific moment. Instead, Beaux carefully arranged the figures on the canvas with the goal of a balanced, well-organized painting. Like Bonheur and Gentileschi, she used classical composition tools. As one example, find the point halfway across the top. A vertical line dropped from it goes through Dorothea and follows the midline of her dress. It's also the starting point for a line that defines the angle of Francesca's leg. Beaux used thirds to guide the design as well: the floor meets the background about where the bottom third meets the middle third, and Dorothea's waistline is on the line between the middle and the upper third. It's also important to note that the canvas's long shape is part of the composition. It perfectly frames the figures against the background.

Lights and Darks

Squinting will help you see that the whole picture is simply a big light shape (figures), a big dark shape (behind them), and a middle gray shape (the floor). The dark background adds a somewhat gloomy note, while the soft lighting suggests the figures are near a window on a cloudy day.

Color

While the grayish background and soft light set a somber mood, Beaux cheered it up with lots of soft, warm pink. Without the pink, the painting is basically monochromatic. This shows how a single color note can dramatically change the mood of a painting.

Adding It Up

Beaux's soft painting style, lifelike drawing, and subtle use of light and color gently disguise the strong structure beneath her composition. Although on first glance this figure painting looks loose and spontaneous, it was carefully planned.

About Cecilia Beaux

Cecilia Beaux didn't want to be called a "woman artist." She wanted to be known for her painting.

Beaux's mother died just days after Beaux was born in 1855 in Philadelphia, Pennsylvania. Her father left the United States after his wife's death and returned to France. Beaux and her sister stayed and were raised by their grandmother, who encouraged creativity, art, music—and hard work.

Beaux showed talent early, and first worked making careful sketches of fossils. She also painted portraits on porcelain, a kind of china, and specialized in portraits, many of her family, during her long and successful career.

Few art schools accepted women students. Beaux was lucky to live near the Pennsylvania Academy of the Fine Arts, one of the only American art schools that allowed women to enroll.

After her portrait of her sister and nephew, *Les Derniers Jours d'Enfance (The Last Days of Infancy)*, won a prize—for the best by a woman—at a Pennsylvania

Academy show, she decided to enter it in the 1887 Paris Salon and move to Paris to study.

After she returned to the United States, she became a successful portrait painter who received numerous commissions. Among her famous sitters was Edith Roosevelt, the wife of President Theodore Roosevelt. Her expertise earned her a teaching position at the Pennsylvania Academy, as its first woman instructor.

She never married. She wanted to be independent and self-sufficient.

Yet like other artists who happened to be women, Beaux couldn't escape being recognized first as a woman and then as an artist. One famous male artist, William Merritt Chase, praised her composition, her use of color, and her style, comparing her to Rembrandt and the Spanish painter Diego Velázquez. He said she was "not only the greatest living woman painter, but the best that has ever lived."

She maintained, instead, that "success is sexless."

Cecilia Beaux died in 1942 at her summer home in Gloucester, Massachusetts.

Lluïsa Vidal Puig, *Self-Portrait*, circa 1899. Oil on canvas, approx. 11 × 14 in. (28.0 × 35.6 cm). Museu Nacional d'Art de Catalunya, donated by Francesca Vidal and other brothers of the artist, 1935. © Museu Nacional d'Art de Catalunya, Barcelona, 2022. Photo credit: Museu Nacional d'Art de Catalunya.

CHAPTER 9

Lluïsa Vidal

Arrive

In this small self-portrait we see Lluïsa Vidal from the waist up. Her body turns toward her easel, while her face turns to a mirror to meet her own eyes—and ours. She has filled her brush with red and is deciding where to dab it.

Explore

Let's take this painting apart and put it back together. It's rich in art lessons.

- What is a simple way Vidal might have approached painting this self-portrait?
- How do the values and colors work together in this painting?

Composition

Vidal probably used the *direct* painting method. Starting with simple color blocks would have helped Vidal easily lock in the general design without a preliminary sketch or underpainting. Notice the four color shapes made by the green wall, the rose smock, Vidal's head, and the black background. After painting these blocks, Vidal would have turned to details like her facial features and the folds of her smock.

Lights and Darks

This painting has dark, middle, and light values, and each takes up a different amount of space. Most of the painting, including parts of the dress, face, palette, and green wall are a middle value; they would match about the same gray on a value scale (see the appendix, p. 175). The painting's dark values take up less space than its middle values. The middle and dark values help create depth: the black background contrasting with warm rose causes Vidal's left shoulder to pop forward, while her right shoulder fades into the green background because there is no value contrast there. Highlight values take up little space, dancing across Vidal's shoulder, hands, and cheek. They enliven the painting, focus attention on the face, and make the shapes more three-dimensional.

Colors

Rose and green are approximately opposite hues on a color wheel (see the appendix, p. 176). Opposite hues are referred to as *complementary colors*, and when two complementary colors appear together, their value, chroma, and temperature determine which color will stand out. Here, the rose and green have about the same value and chroma, but temperature makes the warm rose smock stand out against the cooler green.

Vidal used a limited palette: green, red, and yellow against black. To keep within this color group, she even used green in the skin and fabric shadows.

Adding It Up

By building on a simple composition of color shapes, Vidal crafted a small and realistic self-portrait with personality. She used a limited palette, soft brushstrokes, and contrasts of value, temperature, and hue. Subtle color shifts and highlights created believable plays of light across her face and body.

About Lluïsa Vidal

Lluïsa Vidal painted such vibrant, energetic images that her work was criticized for being too masculine. "She paints so well . . . she paints like a man!" it was said. Vidal supported herself and her extended family through painting and magazine illustration. She also founded her own art academy, where she taught drawing and painting.

Born in Barcelona, Spain, in 1876, Vidal came from a family that valued creativity. Her grandfather headed a workshop that employed fine craftsmen, and her father, who trained in Paris, was a highly regarded cabinetmaker and interior designer. She was one of nine daughters, all of whom were encouraged to pursue creative lives, whether artistic or musical. The young cellist Pablo Casals, who later gained worldwide fame, was one of their teachers. Vidal's father brought her to the Prado Museum in Madrid, where she learned by copying its masterpieces.

At a time when young Spanish women required escorts wherever they went, Vidal took the unusually bold step, at age 25, of moving to Paris by herself. There she attended the Académie Julian. Her dynamic painting made her a sought-after portrait artist, commissioned to paint the likenesses of society elites. Besides portraits, she painted naturalistic, everyday street scenes and domestic interiors with lively, fresh brushstrokes and showed her work in exhibitions in Spain and internationally.

In Barcelona, Vidal cofounded and illustrated a feminist women's magazine, *Feminal*, which was connected with the modernist art movement.

Vidal devoted herself to painting and never married. She died in 1918 during the Spanish flu epidemic.

Angel De Cora (Hinųk Mą̱xiwi Kerenąka), *Josephine Sampson Greyhair*, circa 1904. Oil on canvas, 16 × 14 in. (40.6 × 35.6 cm). Museum of Nebraska Art, Kearney, Nebraska; museum purchase made possible by Jim & Joyce Holtmeier, Julie Morsman Schroeder Foundation, Carl & Karen Brasee, Anne Thorne Weaver; conservation made possible by Maria J. Scott and Julie Morsman Schroeder Foundation. Photo credit: Museum of Nebraska Art, Kearney, Nebraska.

CHAPTER 10

Angel De Cora

Arrive

We arrive at a profile of a woman from the Winnebago Tribe, the artist's half sister Josephine Sampson Greyhair. Painted around 1904, the woman's expression and the dark tones of the painting evoke a serious feeling.

Explore

While we've looked at several portraits, this one is different in subject, format, and style. Unlike the other portraits, it's a *profile*, showing the subject's face in a side view, and it was painted in a *tonalist* style. Let's explore:

- What does the portrait tell us that is new to our painting story?
- What are the artistic challenges of the profile format?
- What is tonalism?

A Unique Painting Story

In the 19th century, painters in Europe and the United States were almost exclusively White. Few individuals from other cultures had opportunities to study painting. Angel De Cora, a Native American from the Winnebago Tribe, was an exception. She studied art in elite White institutions because she had been taken from her Native community involuntarily in her youth.

Painting a Profile

Every view of the face is an artistic challenge, and profiles are no exception. A profile has to start with a properly drawn head and neck. Next, all the details must be right. These include the the positions and shapes of the features and the depth of the eye sockets. In De Cora's beautiful side view, the head has volume, and we can sense how the neck supports the head and connects into the shoulders. Features are placed and drawn correctly. The nose, mouth, and ears seem like those of a real individual. Indeed, the features, earrings, and clothing depict a woman so specific that we could recognize her if we saw her.

Color and Light

De Cora trained in tonalism, which emphasized subtle color and value in dim light. Tonalist painters used shades of brown and gray and other hues of similar value. This portrait reflects De Cora's training with its limited range of value and hue and absence of bright highlights.

Adding It Up

De Cora's solemn portrait communicates Greyhair's cultural background and beauty through realistic design and tonalism. While we celebrate De Cora as a Native American painter, it's important to remember that her life as an artist reflected her personal tragedy. Yet in her art she was able to celebrate her heritage.

About Angel De Cora

In her autobiography, Angel De Cora spoke with fondness of her "ideal" childhood, spending summers on the Winnebago reservation in Nebraska, where she was born in 1871, and winters "moving camp" along rivers and forests. Much of her childhood, she was raised by her grandfather, a hereditary leader of the tribe, who explained to Angel her ancestral traditions. One translation of her Winnebago name, Hinųk Mąxiwi Kerenąka, is "She Returns to the Sky."

Her grandfather had great plans for her, she knew, but she could not know that she would spend her life far from home.

De Cora's happy life changed forever when, in 1883, she and six other children were approached by a White man who asked if they'd like a train ride. She did not know that she was being taken to a boarding school for Native Americans in Hampton, Virginia, funded by the federal government. De Cora would not see her devastated family for three years.

At the boarding school, children were prohibited from speaking their languages and were made to wear uniforms and study the Christian religion. Girls learned sewing and crocheting and worked in the school laundry. The school attempted to assimilate students into the dominant culture by placing them in homes during the summer where they were expected to do household chores. At one home in Massachusetts, De Cora was given private art lessons.

After she graduated from the Hampton school, De Cora attended a girls' boarding school in Northampton,

Massachusetts, and later Smith College. She worked in Smith's art gallery in exchange for tuition and studied with landscape painter Dwight William Tryon, whose quiet tonal landscapes and seascapes influenced her work. She later studied with popular illustrator Howard Pyle at Philadelphia's Drexel Institute. He complained that her art stuck too closely to her heritage. Though their approaches to art differed—"I am Indian and I don't want to draw just like a white man," she was said to have told him—he had high regard for her abilities. "I now feel that Miss de Cora has not only talent but genius," he wrote. "Out of a thousand people ten have genius; she's one of the ten."

While in Philadelphia, De Cora became friends with Cecilia Beaux, who taught at the Pennsylvania Academy of the Fine Arts. She and Beaux had studios in the same Chestnut Street building. At Boston's Museum of Fine Arts, De Cora studied with well-known Impressionist painters Frank Benson and Edmund C. Tarbell. She then moved to New York and worked in illustration, portraiture, and design.

De Cora felt pulled between wishing to pursue landscape painting and making a living through design. She designed and illustrated books on Native American topics, stylizing traditional designs from several traditions. She wrote and illustrated two semiautobiographical stories for the widely read *Harper's Magazine*, "The Sick Child," and "Gray Wolf's Daughter," about a girl who leaves home and traditions behind to attend a White boarding school. She signed those artworks with her traditional name and an abbreviated version of her translated name.

De Cora exhibited paintings at several shows, including the 1893 World's Columbian Exposition in Chicago, the 1901 Pan-American Exposition in Buffalo, and the 1904 St. Louis World's Fair. As the first instructor of Native American art at the Carlisle Indian School in Pennsylvania, she encouraged her students to learn about, take pride in, and practice the traditional arts of their varied cultures. Her activism to honor her heritage included speaking in 1911 at the first meeting of the Society of American Indians, for which she designed a logo and of which she was a member. The conference was centered around the theme of social justice and was purposely held on Columbus Day in Columbus, Ohio. De Cora argued that Americans should understand Native American designs and accurately represent them.

De Cora worked with her husband, whom she met at Carlisle and married in 1908, on several illustration projects. In 1915, she left Carlisle and her husband, and moved to Northampton.

Angel De Cora died of influenza and pneumonia in 1919 in Northampton, Massachusetts.

PART II

Modern Painting

By the end of the 19th century, painters were exploring the limits of realism and experimenting with new ways to use color, line, and shape. Instead of realistic techniques that created the illusion of depth and volume, modern compositions began to emphasize the flat surface of a painting or drawing. Some modern artists rejected representation completely. They embraced pure abstraction, using energetic lines and fields of color not to realistically portray identifiable objects but to express ideas and feelings directly through paint. Although Paris at first was the center of the modern art movement, New York City later became the hub. By the mid-20th century, painting had been completely transformed from its classical roots in Europe hundreds of years earlier. While many artists continued to practice realism, others, no longer bound by tradition, explored and developed materials, subjects, formats, and techniques that let them express themselves freely.

Suzanne Valadon, *Self-Portrait*, 1898. Oil on canvas,
15¾ × 10½ in. (40.0 × 26.7 cm). The Museum of Fine
Arts, Houston, Texas, USA; museum purchase funded
by Audrey Jones Beck. Copyright © Museum of Fine
Arts, Houston, Texas. Photo credit: Bridgeman Images.

CHAPTER 11

Suzanne Valadon

Arrive

This small painting has a loud voice. Everything about this self-portrait is assertive, strong, and fearless, as if the subject and artist, Suzanne Valadon, doesn't care about our opinion. Though she appears very real and full of personality, the painting is not realistic in the way we got used to seeing in part 1. Think about the effect this painting has on you. How much of that effect comes from the style versus the subject?

Explore

Suzanne Valadon's self-portrait is different from every other painting we've looked at so far. It brings us to the beginning of modernism. Let's take a closer look at how Suzanne Valadon's famous self-portrait works.

- In what ways is it modern?
- What gives it so much energy?

Composition and Design

Valadon centered the face and placed her mouth, the boldest part of the painting, directly in the middle of the small canvas. She's turned very slightly to one side. It's a simple, classical angle.

The rest is not at all classical. This painting is full of bold, energetic lines. Look at Valadon's eyebrows, eyes, nose, and lips. They look more drawn than painted, since she used the paint to outline her features instead of blending it to create realistic surfaces. This breaks from more traditional styles that use paint to create rounded, realistic forms. Valadon's heavy lines flatten the face and almost make it mask-like.

Light and Color

Valadon's use of value makes a simple statement. She gives us a pale face and neck against a dark dress, dark hair, and dark background. While the value contrast is strong, it's color hue and intensity that really carry the painting. What color is bolder than red? It's every-where: in the dress, hair, background, and lips.

Yet red isn't the only intense color at play. Valadon brings other hues to her face, with bright blue eyes, pink cheeks, and yellow highlights. Notice the way she used green on the forehead and in other shaded areas of her face. Green and red are complementary colors; putting them near each other makes them each a little louder. The colors aren't natural, but they are courageous.

Adding It Up

In this bold self-portrait, nothing is subtle, sentimental, or highly detailed. It sweeps us into the modern era of painting with simplicity, color, and feeling. More traditional representational works used paint to create depth and form and realistic skin, hair, and fabric. Valadon used paint to create personality.

About Suzanne Valadon

Unlike many of the successful women artists who preceded her, Suzanne Valadon came from a humble background and was self-taught. Born in Paris in 1865 and named Marie-Clémentine by her washerwoman mother, she was considered unruly as a child, which led her mother to enroll her in a religious school. At 14, she left her regimented school in Montmartre, finding employment as a seamstress, fruit seller, dishwasher, and stable hand and then as a circus stunt rider and trapeze artist.

After a fall from the trapeze, Marie-Clémentine sketched while she recovered. Unable to perform and infatuated with art, she became an artists' model. She posed for well-known artists such as Henri de Toulouse-Lautrec, who called her "Suzanne," and Auguste Renoir, who featured Valadon in several of his paintings, including *Dance at Bougival* and *Dance in the Country*. While she posed, she paid close attention to their techniques, learning the art of capturing the figure. Her own artwork focused on drawing intimate family scenes between mothers and their young children, including portraits of her son, Maurice Utrillo. Later, he too became a painter.

She was encouraged to move from drawing to painting by artist Andre Utter, whom she later married. She regularly exhibited in the Paris salons. Rather than paint in the Impressionist style favored by near-contemporaries such as Mary Cassatt and Berthe Morisot, Valadon painted works that express modernity and reject sentimentality. In their composition, palette, and technique, her paintings portray strength and individuality.

Valadon's work was celebrated in Paris and internationally, and she, Utter, and Utrillo were featured in a 1930 show at New York's Demotte Galleries. When Pablo Picasso viewed her art at Paris's Salon d'Automne, he was reported to have said, "If I were to purchase something here, it would be the picture by Suzanne Valadon."

Valadon died of a stroke in Paris in 1938.

Paula Modersohn-Becker, *Still Life with Goldfish Bowl*,
1906. Oil on canvas, 19⅞ × 29⅛ in. (50.5 × 74.0 cm). Found
in the collection of Von der Heydt Museum, Wuppertal,
Germany. Photo credit: HIP / Art Resource, NY.

CHAPTER 12

Paula Modersohn-Becker

Arrive

Three goldfish have paused within their crowded bowl. The space is so small that when one moves they must all move, and when one pauses they must all pause. In this moment of stillness they look around at their surroundings. As viewers we too look around, enjoying the bright colors and curving shapes.

Explore

In *Still Life with Goldfish Bowl*, our eyes circle the urn, bounce among the fruit, and zigzag through the goldfish. The bright colors energize the solid-looking shapes. Although the painting looks playful, it is also serious, because it represents the artist's bold rejection of traditional realism. Let's explore:

- How did Paula Modersohn-Becker structure the painting?
- How did she use color and shape to express her individual ideas?

Structure and Play

Modersohn-Becker arranged her still life to feel organized yet lively. The sense of organization comes from the painting's underlying structure, beginning with the horizontal table edge and the verticals in the urn handle and goldfish bowl pedestal. The outside curves of the urn and fishbowl add more structure by containing the arrangement, providing symmetry, and holding our attention on what's between them.

Color and Shape

The colors and shapes work together to express the artist's ideas about her arrangement.

The shapes show Modersohn-Becker's drive to free herself from realism. Many of them are not quite "right." The urn is lopsided, and the table edge isn't level. The fruits seem too big for their bowl and the fish too big compared to the fruit. Although the fruit bowl casts a shadow, the urn and goldfish bowl do not. These are not errors. Modersohn-Becker let go of accuracy when it interfered with her ideas. She was looking for expressive color and shape relationships; perfect drawing would only lead to a dull repetition of centuries of tradition. Although the painting is not realistic, the artist did lean on a traditional idea in still life: *theme and variation.* Themes create unity, and variation creates interest. Modersohn-Becker created a color theme from red, orange, yellow, and gold—all happy colors, and all analogous hues on the color wheel. To make them stand out, she placed them against gray draperies, creating contrasts of value, chroma, and temperature. Look for examples of light against dark, bright against dull, and warm against cool.

We can also observe two shape themes. Almost all the shapes are round or oval and in a group of three. See if you can find other "triplets" in addition to the goldfish. For variety, the shapes differ in width, height, and how they cluster together. The one exception is the pink flower, whose shape and color break free of the painting's themes.

Adding It Up

Still Life with Goldfish Bowl demonstrates that Modersohn-Becker's formal art training was a springboard for self-expression. She used her design, drawing, and color skills to free herself from simply painting what she saw. Are there symbols in the painting of feeling trapped and feeling free? Consider the goldfish in their bowl, and the small pink flower.

About Paula Modersohn-Becker

Paula Modersohn-Becker's landscapes, portraits, and figure paintings are imbued with emotion. She wanted her work to express an inner feeling rather than an impression or rendering of a particular scene or person. Her modern, simplified shapes and swaths of color represent, rather than detail, objects, people, or landscapes, yet unlike completely abstract works, each element is clearly identifiable.

Born in 1876 in Dresden, Germany, Modersohn-Becker began drawing early, and her parents encouraged her artistic efforts. At age 16, she spent several months living with her aunt near London, where she began drawing from plaster models of the human body. She began studying to become a teacher but soon focused on her passion for art. She studied with a painter in Bremen, Germany, using charcoal to draw live models, and then at a women's art school in Berlin. She was deepening her ability to see like an artist.

"Whenever I talk with somebody I try hard to see just what kind of shadow his or her nose casts," she wrote to her parents in 1896, "or how the deep shadow under a certain cheekbone starts out and then gradually blends into the highlights."

After her family visited the Worpswede, Germany, art colony, she returned for a month of art-making. She painted her first *plein-air* portrait, working outdoors directly from nature, and was dazzled by the experience. Throughout her short career, she would go on to create more than 400 portrait and figural paintings, including dozens of self-portraits and nudes and about 70 still lifes.

Modersohn-Becker steeped herself in art, visiting museums in Dresden and Vienna and viewing Impressionist works by Degas, Monet, and Camille Pissarro. She saw her move to Worpswede to study as temporary. "I am savouring my life with every breath I draw, and in the distance Paris gleams and shimmers," she wrote to her aunt. "I truly believe that my most secret and ardent wish is going to come true."

Modersohn-Becker visited Paris six times during her short life, five times after her 1901 marriage to painter Otto Modersohn. There she discovered the work of Paul Cézanne, with its geometric blocks of color. It was a turning point for her, and the color in her still lifes show his influence. She also attended life drawing classes at Paris's Académie Colarossi, took anatomy sessions at the École des Beaux-Arts, drew at the Louvre, and discovered artists in galleries and museums. She intended to make Paris the center of her artistic life.

Her family disapproved. "Your two letters . . . made you sound so dissatisfied with me. I, too, can see no end to the whole thing," she wrote to her father during her first stay in Paris. "I must calmly follow my path, and when I get to where I can accomplish something, things will be better. None of you, to be sure, seems to have much faith in me. But I do."

In 1907 Paula Modersohn-Becker died of a blood clot just three weeks after giving birth to her daughter.

Activity 4: Experiment with Negative Shapes

The object you draw is a positive shape, and the shape around it is negative. Negative shapes are part of drawing or painting, so practice making them work for you. Paula Modersohn-Becker's still life has many interesting positive and negative shapes. Other good examples are in the paintings by Rachel Ruysch (p. 16) and Alma Thomas (p. 160). Ruysch's bouquet has a shape, and so does the background that touches it. Thomas's red shape has another shape around it.

You'll Need

Pencil and eraser
Paper
Favorite painting supplies

1. Place a simple object, like a bottle or piece of fruit, on a table. Make a sketch.
2. Make a new sketch. Instead of sketching the object itself, look at the spaces around it, and draw those shapes. See if your object shows up on your paper!
3. Try a more complicated object when you're ready, like a chair or lamp.
4. Repeat this with paint. Notice how you can paint the object or paint the space around it.

Angelina Beloff, *Vista de Toledo (View of Toledo),*
circa 1913. Oil on canvas on wood, 31½ × 25⅝ in.
(80 × 65 cm). Colección Andres Blaisten,
México. Photo credit: Museo Blaisten.

CHAPTER 13

Angelina Beloff

Arrive

Modern artists like Angelina Beloff experimented with alternatives to realistic portrayals of the world. Her view of Toledo, Spain, is recognizable yet abstract. It has two main areas: a small sky and a big landscape. A town sits on top of the land. Below, a bridge slices across, its enormous arch dominating the center. Then in the foreground the landscape abruptly falls apart. We are left questioning what we see, which might be exactly what Angelina Beloff wanted.

Explore

Many artists have painted realistic views of the ancient bridges that span the Tagus River at Toledo, Spain. Angelina Beloff's interpretation, most likely of the Puente de

Alcántara, stepped away from realism. Take a minute to familiarize yourself (don't miss the sheep). Then, let's explore:

- How did Beloff use traditional landscape "rules"?
- How did she break away from traditional landscape design?
- How did she use color and brushstrokes?

Design

Beloff's design keeps our attention on the bridge's arch and the orange streak below it. The bridge stops our eyes from moving further into the painting, encouraging us to figure out the foreground.

A different way to look at the painting is possible. Start at the bottom and go *through* the arch to the top of the hill. Suddenly, the painting tells a different story. The town is the focus and the pink tower in the upper right is the vanishing point, with several lines of perspective leading to it. Try to find at least four of these lines within the landscape. Beloff used traditional linear perspective unconventionally, encouraging us to wander before finding our way.

This interpretation helps explain the foreground. If you were at your easel looking up at Toledo, everything below would be outside your focus. You would have a blurry sense of the dizzy drop to the river but would not see it in detail. Beloff may have been trying to paint the way we see: our eyes can only focus on one place at a time.

Painting Vista de Toledo

To create the mysterious foreground and clear background, Beloff repeated the same colors while varying her brushwork throughout. The foreground strokes are larger and more vertical, while small, neat marks form the houses and buildings. Warm colors fill the ravine and the building fronts. Perhaps this is twilight, and the buildings, rocks, and water are reflecting sunset's colors.

Adding It Up

Vista de Toledo is a complicated image that reveals its secrets slowly. In a way, this painting flips the usual order in a landscape by placing clarity in the background. While Beloff used traditional elements— linear perspective and foreground, midground, and background—she disrupted our expectations. *Vista de Toledo* challenges our ideas about what "should" happen in a landscape.

About Angelina Beloff

Born in Saint Petersburg, Russia, in 1879, Angelina Beloff lived mostly in France and in Mexico, which was her home for more than 30 years. Encouraged by her parents to explore her artistic talent, before leaving Russia she studied at the Saint Petersburg Academy of Arts, where she earned a license to teach drawing. At age 30 she made her way to the center of European art—Paris.

In Paris she painted landscapes and portraits, some of them featuring Mexican painters who had come to Paris to study. She studied with Henri Matisse and Spanish painter Hermenegildo Anglada Camarasa, and the influence of their unnatural palettes and thick layers of paint are evident in her much later work *Vista de Toledo*. Beloff exhibited at the Salon des Indepéndants from 1912 to 1930.

On a visit to Bruges, Belgium, with Spanish Cubist painter María Blanchard, she met the Mexican muralist Diego Rivera. When they met, Beloff and Rivera didn't speak each other's languages, but they fell in love and lived together in France for 10 years. They shared their home and studio in Montparnasse with Blanchard. They had a son, who died when he was not yet two years old.

In 1914 she, Rivera, Blanchard, and other artist friends took a sketching tour of Spain. Beloff's work there showed the influence of Cézanne's color palette and simplified shapes. Beloff was the subject of a number of Rivera's portraits, ranging from realistic to simplified geometric shapes in a style called Cubism. In 1921 he left her to go to Mexico. Though she expected him to return, he did not, and he married the artist Frida Kahlo a few years later.

Beloff moved to Mexico City in 1932. Private art galleries had just begun to spring up in a culture where murals, mostly painted by men, were a dominant art form. Frida Kahlo was one of the earliest women to show her work there, in 1929.

Angelina Beloff used her artistic talents in many ways: she taught art, founded a gallery, illustrated books, created woodcuts, made marionettes and promoted puppet theaters as effective methods of teaching children, and continued painting. In 1945 she was awarded a coveted commission to paint a mural. More than 200 of her works were exhibited at the Palacio de Bellas Artes in Mexico City.

Angelina Beloff died in Mexico in 1969.

Tarsila do Amaral, *A Família*, 1925. Oil on canvas, 31⅛ ×
40 in. (79.0 × 101.5 cm). Museo Nacional Centro de Arte
Reina Sofía. Image copyright © Tarsila do Amaral. Photo
credit: Museo Nacional Centro de Arte Reina Sofía.

CHAPTER 14

Tarsila do Amaral

Arrive

Arriving at this painting feels like entering a family gathering in full swing. Five children and seven grown-ups crowd into the canvas along with a cat, a dog, a doll, and what might be a bunch of bananas. Tarsila (the artist used her first name professionally) created a sense of energy and restraint, as if everyone is trying to hold still just long enough for a photograph.

Explore

Painted in 1925, *A Familia* is a modern twist on an old subject. Tarsila's arrangement of simple, repetitive shapes captures an authentic feeling about this family gathering, and it's another example of an artist moving away from realism. Let's explore:

- What kind of energy did Tarsila create in this painting, and how did she do it?
- How did Tarsila use the theme of repetition?

Design

The energy of *A Familia* brings to mind harmony inter-mixed with chaos, like the way a family really is. The composition seems as if the arrangement would fly apart if anyone moved.

The sense of harmony comes partly from the balanced design. The boy with the fruit grounds the painting in the middle. The others surround him in an example of *asymmetrical balance*: though Tarsila didn't mirror the left and right halves, they have the same visual weight.

Tarsila's repetitive shapes and colors add to the sense of harmony. The heads, for example, are all simple and circular. She used few colors, repeating each with careful attention to where she placed it. The three white shirts, for example, form a symmetrical group around the middle. Likewise, Tarsila carefully distributed the pink, blue, and tan hues, adding a single pop of yellow in the fruit.

With all that harmony, why does *A Familia* also burst with energy? It's because the repetitive figures are close to each other and close to the frame. As a result, your eyes bounce around the heads and against the edges. Movement swirls around and around, as well as up and out. Looking at this painting is an exciting experience.

Adding It Up

Tarsila took the complicated idea of painting 12 people, two pets, a doll, and some fruit and simplified it using a balanced design based on repetitive shapes and colors. By packing the canvas with information, Tarsila created a harmonious yet restless energy.

About Tarsila do Amaral

Considered the inventor of modern Brazilian painting, Tarsila do Amaral's most famous works are rooted in Brazilian culture. The daughter of a wealthy coffee plantation owner, she was born in 1886 and grew up in the countryside near São Paulo. Educated at a religious school in Brazil, she studied at a convent school in Barcelona, Spain, where in 1904 she produced her first painting, *Sagrado Coração de Jesus (The Sacred Heart of Jesus)*, a copy of a classical European work. The somber hues of her faithful and skilled copy give no hint of the vibrant art that she would later produce.

Tarsila studied sculpture, painting, and drawing, and from 1920 to 1922 attended the Académie Julian in Paris, which produced many modern painters. The work she created in Paris shows the influence of her training and the extent of her talents. Some portraits, landscapes, and cityscapes employ loose brushstrokes in the French Impressionist style; others confidently present portrait subjects in a modern style with a limited, strongly colored palette.

When Tarsila returned to Brazil, she found her artist friends had been inspired by a recent modernist exhibition that sparked a new type of painting. She became part of the "Group of Five," dedicated to popularizing modernism.

Returning to the Académie Julian in 1923, she experimented with Cubism in portraiture and landscape, influenced by Cubist painter Fernand Léger and visits to Pablo Picasso's studio. This new modernism sparked the creation of her own signature style.

In a 1923 letter to her parents, written from Paris, she resolved to become "the painter of my country." Tarsila meshed modernism with aspects of Brazilian Indigenous culture, yet she experienced that culture as a woman of privilege. Her boldly colored, dreamlike landscapes, figure paintings with exaggerated human forms, and incorporation of traditional designs from

Brazilian culture made her work exciting and unique. Dubbed "anthropophagic" for its intellectual process of digesting Western culture and transforming it into something new, Tarsila achieved her goal of becoming the premier painter of Brazil.

The 1929 stock market crash, which kicked off the Great Depression worldwide, dramatically changed Tarsila's economic status. She continued to challenge accepted notions of art as she took on political and social themes in her work. She was even jailed for her involvement in communism.

Of her inspiration to create a Brazilian style, Tarsila said: "I found in Minas [a southeastern Brazilian state] the colors I used to love as a child. I was subsequently taught that these colors were ugly and of poor taste, but afterwards I avenged the oppression by incorporating them in my paintings: the purest blue, purplish pink, bright yellow, singing green."

Tarsila do Amaral died in São Paulo in 1973.

Laura Wheeler Waring, *Anna Washington Derry*, 1927. Oil on canvas, 20 × 16 in. (50.8 × 40.5 cm). Smithsonian American Art Museum, Washington, DC, gift of the Harmon Foundation. Photo credit: Smithsonian American Art Museum, Washington, DC / Art Resource, NY.

CHAPTER 15

Laura Wheeler Waring

Arrive

Laura Wheeler Waring's portrait of Anna Washington Derry, whom Waring knew from her local community in Pennsylvania, exemplifies the artist's honest, sensitive approach. With loose brushwork and strong negative shapes, Waring's style is modern yet realistic. Here, Anna Derry rests, her arms calmly crossed and her gaze soft and thoughtful.

Explore

This painting radiates stability and peace. Let's identify three aspects of Waring's technique that contribute to this feeling.

- How did Waring use positive and negative shapes?
- How did Waring use value and color?
- What techniques did Waring use to render Anna Derry's expression so realistically?

Design

Artists often use triangles to simplify portrait and figure design. Here, the whole figure is a triangle. Anna Derry's crossed arms form the base across the bottom, her arms form the sides, and her head is at the top. The figure's broad base adds both spatial and emotional weight to the painting—it looks heavier at the bottom, and feels grounded and stable. Interestingly, additional triangles may be found nested inside the figure, a unifying design theme.

Value and Color

In *Anna Washington Derry*, value and color work together. The portrait is almost monochromatic, relying on gray and brown tones that vary between the black hair to the highlights on the collar and cuffs. The color and value scheme are gentle and quiet, setting a calm mood. If you squint, you can simplify the painting to three tones: the pale background and dress trim, the middle value in the dress and shadow, and the dark value of the skin and hair. Waring paid close attention to crafting beautiful negative shapes, especially around the head, using value contrasts. Look, for example, at the shape the gold background makes going around the head and its shadow.

Portrait details

Waring painted the background and dress loosely, using more detailed brushwork on Anna Derry's hands and face. These main features were painted realistically and with patient attention to the way light reflected differently off of each of the hollows, angles, and curves of the hands, fingers, and face. On the face, Waring's cool bluish highlights and warm shadows delicately model the sitter's features and bring her calm expression to life.

Adding It Up

Waring's portrait demonstrates how a monochromatic color scheme can create a calm mood. Her careful combination of large positive and negative shapes with fine details in the face and hands achieve an astonishing simplicity and perfection. Anna Washington Derry almost seems about to breathe or sigh while she patiently waits for the artist to finish.

About Laura Wheeler Waring

Laura Wheeler Waring was born in 1887 in Hartford, Connecticut. Her father was a pastor, and her mother, an amateur artist, was a graduate of Oberlin College, the first US college to enroll Black students.

Waring studied at the Pennsylvania Academy of the Fine Arts, which was known for encouraging women artists. In 1914 she received the academy's highest honor, a scholarship that allowed her to study in Paris. In 1928 she was awarded a national honor from the Harmon Foundation, which recognized the achievements of Black creatives in a variety of fields, including fine arts. Her work was exhibited in its first show to focus solely on Black artists. She made several trips to Europe to study painting.

Waring specialized in portrait painting and received widespread recognition for her Harmon Foundation project depicting noteworthy figures such as abolitionist Harriet Tubman and opera singer Marian Anderson. First Lady Eleanor Roosevelt attended the show's 1944 opening and praised the works in her daily news column.

Those paintings, produced later in her career, are bold and dramatic and showcase the larger-than-life aspect of these heroes and their monumental impact on society. In contrast, her portrait of Anna Washington Derry is quiet, thoughtful, and understated. Like many artists, Waring painted people she knew. Anna Washington Derry was a working-class woman whose son was groundskeeper at the school where Waring taught. This portrait received a gold medal from the Harmon Foundation.

Waring was involved in the Harlem Renaissance through her work for the magazine *Crisis*, published by the civil rights organization the NAACP and edited by civil rights activist W. E. B. Du Bois. The Harlem Renaissance was a cultural movement that led to an outpouring of art, music, and literature from African Americans. Du Bois recognized that this new wave of Black artists could help advance the civil rights agenda, so his magazine addressed racism but also celebrated Black Americans' artistic achievements. Highlighting works by Black women artists in particular was part of that recognition. Waring was the magazine's most prolific artistic contributor, illustrating articles, short stories, and poems and creating covers that featured silhouetted figures and included African- and Egyptian-inspired designs.

Waring taught for almost 40 years at the Cheyney Training School for Teachers (now Cheyney University) near Philadelphia, the first school of higher learning for African Americans, and became head of its art and music department. She married Walter Waring, a professor at Lincoln University in Pennsylvania, when she was 40 years old. She had no children.

Laura Wheeler Waring died in Philadelphia in 1948.

Activity 5: Draw Better Faces

Laura Wheeler Waring's portrait is realistic and expressive. A portrait painting starts with a good drawing, but drawing faces is hard. This activity will help.

You'll Need

Pencil and eraser
Paper
Ruler
A person's face, either your own in a mirror or one in a photograph—or you could ask a friend to pose for you

1. Study your subject for at least five minutes without drawing anything. Make sure the head is straight and facing you.
2. Sketch your subject for 10 to 15 minutes. Include the head, face, hair, and neck. Add ears if they are visible.
3. Now start a fresh drawing. Lightly draw an oval for the head. Add the neck, carefully looking at how wide it is compared to the head.
4. Now use a ruler to *lightly* draw two lines. Draw a vertical axis down the middle of the head from top to chin. Draw a horizontal axis for the eyes; to figure out where to draw it, notice the eyes are about halfway between the top of the head and the chin.
5. Use the axis lines to place the features. Center the nose, mouth, and chin on the vertical axis. Draw the eyes, placing the pupils on the horizontal axis. The distance between the eyes is about the length of an eye. Draw the ears, if they are visible, noticing that their tops are at or just below the horizontal axis. Be mindful of the size of the features, but don't get too caught up in accuracy at first. Erase the axis lines.
6. Add more details, including eyebrows and shadows. Draw the overall shape of the hair before you add any detail to it.
7. How did your original freehand sketch compare to the one with the axis lines?

Amrita Sher-Gil, *Group of Three Girls*, 1935. Oil on canvas, 29 × 39⅛ in. (73.5 × 99.5 cm). National Gallery of Modern Art, New Delhi (accession # 982). Photo credit: National Gallery of Modern Art, New Delhi.

CHAPTER 16

Amrita Sher-Gil

Arrive

In Amrita Sher-Gil's graceful figure composition, three girls sit closely, their forms almost filling the canvas. Their scarves drape them in abstract, richly colored shapes. Our art travels have taken us to India.

Explore

Each girl looks different from the others, yet the whole group works together. As you explore *Group of Three Girls*, notice where your eyes rest and what direction they move in. Let's explore:

- What is the big idea that guides the design?
- How does the big idea affect how we look at the painting?
- How do color and value add to the design idea?

Composition and Design

Amrita Sher-Gil flattened and compressed space in this painting. The girls are close to each other and to the edges, and there is little depth behind them. As in Mary Cassatt's work, this figure group is one big shape. Its curvy outline and the way the artist divided it work together as the big design idea. Its main divisions are the three draped figures. Sher-Gil painted them in a flat and abstract manner; we have little sense of the girls themselves other than as parts of this beautiful shape.

As you look at the girls, your eyes move in and out of the center. Sher-Gil's design is like a pinwheel made of curves that spin us around and meet in the middle. To see this, imagine or lightly trace an *x* from corner to corner. Notice that almost every curve comes out of or into where the hands cross. Notice, too, that *everything* is curved. There are no straight lines or stopping points. Look at the girl on the right. Her crossed hands lead up her arm, over her head, and back to the center.

Light and Color

The figure of the girl on the left is far lighter than the others. Having a big, light shape only on one side could have unbalanced the design. To reestablish balance in the lights and darks, Sher-Gil lit up the right figure's face. This was probably an artistic decision, rather than what she saw. Can you see why? Because light could not fall on this girl's face without lighting the other faces. The design and use of value probably aren't what you first noticed about this painting. It had to be the color! Look at the beautiful reds and how they vary from a pale red-orange to a deep red-violet. They contrast with the refreshing pear color on the left. The faces, hands, and background are in warm shades of brown that let the colors fly out without restraint.

Adding It Up

Though it is a figure painting, the design and rich colors are the main subject. Sher-Gil seems to have been inspired by the abstract shapes formed by the three girls draped in fabric. The girls' faces and hands, though realistic, are a small part of the painting. We are swept up in the pinwheel of color.

About Amrita Sher-Gil

"It seems that I never *began* painting, that I have always painted," Amrita Sher-Gil wrote. "And I have always had, with a strange certitude, the conviction that I was meant to be a painter and nothing else."

Sher-Gil had deep connections on two continents. She was born in Budapest, Hungary, in 1913, and her Hungarian mother was an opera singer and musician. Her father was from India, a multilingual scholar of Persian and Sanskrit who had a deep interest in astronomy and photography.

As a child, Sher-Gil drew and painted constantly, on whatever she could find: scraps of paper, toilet paper, the walls of her home. She was intensely interested in Hungarian fairy tales, illustrating classic versions and writing some of her own.

After her family moved to Simla, India, when Sher-Gil was eight, she worked with an art teacher who made her draw the same subject over and over. She objected, and a new teacher, realizing her talent, encouraged Sher-Gil's parents to give her an artistic education in Europe.

In Florence, Italy, she attended a boarding school, but after six months she was expelled, supposedly for drawing nudes. After she was also expelled from an Indian convent school because she said that she was an atheist, her family moved to Paris so the 16-year-old Sher-Gil could study art at the French academies. There she was the first Indian admitted to the École des Beaux-Arts and the youngest member elected to the Paris Salon. She exhibited there as a teen, a major achievement for someone so young; in 1933 her painting *Young Girls* received the salon's top honors.

Sher-Gil was admired for her portraits, which often used strong reds and vigorous brushstrokes. In turn, she admired Suzanne Valadon's work, as well as that of Vincent van Gogh, Paul Cézanne, and Paul Gauguin. Her work melded modern Western painting with Indian tradition.

Her mother was concerned that she might have had romantic relationships with women, though she denied that and later married a Hungarian man, her cousin.

"Towards the end of 1933, I began to be haunted by an intense longing to return to India, feeling in some strange, inexplicable way that there lay my destiny as a painter," she wrote. In a 1934 letter to her parents, she wrote that "modern art has led me to the comprehension & appreciation of Indian painting and sculpture" that she wouldn't have understood had she not left her home.

She was influenced by traditional Indian miniature paintings and murals that she saw during a trip to South India. On that trip, she painted ordinary scenes and ordinary people and felt it her destiny to honor impoverished people with her art. She resolved "to interpret the life of Indians . . . with a new technique, my own technique."

Amrita Sher-Gil died unexpectedly in 1941, just as a major exhibition of her work was to open. Her paintings have been designated National Art Treasures by the government of India.

Activity 6: Start with Big Shapes

Artists often use a big shape or shapes to anchor their composition. They add the details afterwards. Amrita Sher-Gil's painting has a big shape that contains the three girls. In this activity you'll work with the big shapes in several paintings in this book.

You'll Need

Pencil and eraser
Tracing paper
Favorite painting supplies
Paper

1. Trace the outline of the big shape in Sher-Gil's painting. Take the tracing off the book. Draw on your tracing, trying to copy the way Sher-Gil drew the three girls inside the shape.
2. Now look at Mary Cassatt's painting (p. 46). With your tracing paper, trace the outer edges of the painting (the rectangle), and outline the big shape that includes the figures, bowl, and pitcher.
3. Still tracing, add the lines that separate the forms in the big shape.
4. Now you can start to add details to the tracing.
5. You can also try this activity with the paintings by Lavinia Fontana (p. 2) and Lluïsa Vidal (p. 58). Notice how the artists might have gradually added details to their big shapes.
6. Try it with paints! Let the paint dry after you make the big shapes. Then add the next level of detail and let the paint dry again. Repeat until you have all the detail you want.

Yuki Ogura, *Bathing Women*, 1938. Color on silk.
82⅓ × 68¾ in. (209.0 × 174.5 cm). The National
Museum of Modern Art, Tokyo. © Yuki Ogura / licensed
by TETSUJU Ltd. Photo: MOMAT / DNPartcom.

CHAPTER 17

Yuki Ogura

Arrive

Almost 7 feet by 6 feet, Yuki Ogura's *Bathing Women* throws open the doors to a scene most would consider private. We seem to have stepped into a life-size room where two naked women, comfortably oblivious to our presence, seek rest in the warm waters of a tiled pool. Though the painting is quiet, it's also unconventional, combining delicate lines and color with the power of its size and the boldness of the subject.

Explore

Yuki Ogura's painting is an example of modern Japanese art. It marries traditional Japanese interest in flat space, graceful figures, and uncluttered surfaces with modern interest in freedom of expression and in line, scale, color, and abstract shape. The painting seems very still. One woman, viewed from behind, rests in the water. The other has paused before lowering herself in.

Let's explore:

- How did Ogura paint space?
- How did she paint form?
- How do color, shape, and line work together?

Space Versus Surface

Viewed at its true size, *Bathing Women* might look as if a wall had been removed and we were looking into a room. Line plays an important role in fostering this impression. The sense of depth comes from the artist's use of fine lines to separate the tiles and create perspective. Without the tile lines, the walls and tub would appear completely flat; with the lines included, we know we are looking into a space that has walls, a floor, and a pool with a sloping bottom.

In contrast to the tiles, the figures, as well as the floor, have no features that suggest volume or depth. If you cover the painting except for the floor, that little area will seem flat, not like a surface extending away from you. And in the figures, Ogura's outlines and absence of shading make them appear flat as well.

If we were to trace this painting with pencil lines, we'd see that it is made up of a flat surface design that is mostly simple geometric shapes. This geometric design is punctuated with the graceful curved shapes of the women. The contrast of the flat forms with the lines of perspective in the tiles creates some tension in the painting. The flat surface pattern coexists with illusions of depth.

Line, Color and Shape

Ogura carefully balanced the influence of line, color, and shape. None of these elements dominate the painting, yet all are essential to the experience of looking at the painting. Their unity contributes to the picture's sense of quiet and stillness.

Adding It Up

Bathing Women combines traditional Japanese ideas about painting with modern interests in large-scale works, line, color, and shape. Combining flat shapes and depth of space is an idea other artists also explored in the 20th century, including Maria Leontina (chapter 21, p. 147). The great size of Ogura's painting, in contrast to the comfortable nakedness of the figures, seems to ask us to think about our ideas of privacy.

About Yuki Ogura

Born in Ōtsu, Japan, in 1895, Yuki Ogura didn't plan to be an artist. Yet she painted for most of her life—until the year before she died at age 105.

Ogura melded East and West as she used traditional materials to forge her own art style. She depicted women and children with simplified, modern forms, as in *Bathing Women*.

Ogura's work was influenced by a dramatic change in Japanese art and culture. Traditional Japanese painting, called nihonga, uses materials such as colored inks and pigments from natural materials. Each color is created according to traditional recipes and with specific ingredients, such as oyster shells for white and azurite for blue. The pigments are applied with special brushes on silk or on traditional paper called washi.

An 1868 political revolution opened up Japan to modernize its industry, trade, and culture. In 1889 the Tokyo School of Fine Arts opened and offered studies in Japanese painting, sculpture, and crafts. In 1896—a year after Ogura was born—the school's administrators realized there was a demand for instruction in Western-style painting and created a curriculum based on French academy methods. The goal was to create a foundation in techniques, such as composition and perspective, to inform traditional Japanese art. It resulted in a style that Ogura felt was unoriginal.

At first, Ogura wasn't interested in art, even though her high school teacher encouraged her to go to art school. She studied Chinese and Japanese literature at a women's teachers' college, now Nara Women's University, and took classes in traditional painting and art history. A visit to a biennial exhibition, Inten, at the Japan Art Institute, founded by Yasuda Yukihiko, changed her life. "I have a vivid memory of every single work exhibited by senior artists," she said. "The works at *Inten* were very fresh compared to the works at *Bunten* [government-sponsored exhibitions] which were stale. The germ of my spirit was cultivated at that time by *Inten*."

Ogura began studying with Yasuda Yukihiko. Her first entry into a Japan Art Institute exhibit was rejected, but a still life was accepted the next year, in 1926, and she exhibited every year after that. At 37 she became the first woman accepted as an Art Institute member.

Ogura followed Western art through a Japanese arts magazine, *Shirakaba*, that highlighted artists such as Van Gogh and Cézanne. She attended exhibits, including a major Henri Matisse exhibit in 1951, continually learning and growing as a painter.

As she aged, Ogura painted small still lifes and floral arrangements with vigorous brushwork, and, though suffering from depression, set a goal of completing a painting a month. At 85, she received the prized Order of Culture medal for her artistic achievements; at 95, she was elected president of the Art Institute; at 102, she exhibited two floral paintings; and at 104 she had a solo show in Paris, her first outside Japan.

Yuki Ogura sought to create "Something Bright, Warm, and Pleasant." She died in Kamakura, Japan, in 2000.

Activity 7: Explore Value Contrast

Strong contrasts draw viewers' attention and help emphasize a painting's subject. While Yuki Ogura's painting mostly uses light values, the women's hair is shown as black shapes that stand out. They immediately draw your attention to the women.

You'll Need

Pencil and eraser
Paper
Ruler

1. With your pencil and ruler, make a 3-by-4-inch rectangle.
2. Inside the rectangle, draw a design of squiggles that make lots of enclosed shapes.
3. Using your pencil, fill in most of the shapes, varying how light and dark they are. Leave some of them white. Create one area with strong value contrast between neighboring shapes (black against white). Use smaller value contrasts in the rest of the design—for example, light gray against medium gray; white against light gray.
4. Step back and look. Notice what parts of your design stand out most. How might you use value contrast in your next drawing or painting?

Loïs Mailou Jones, *Self Portrait*, 1940. Casein on board, 17½ × 14½ in. (44.5 × 36.7 cm). Smithsonian American Art Museum, Washington, DC, bequest of the artist (2006.24.2). Photo credit: Smithsonian American Art Museum, Washington, DC / Art Resource, NY.

CHAPTER 18

Loïs Mailou Jones

Arrive

The artist stands alone at her easel, appearing to look at us while actually looking into a mirror. Lluïsa Vidal and Suzanne Valadon took up the same challenge using different styles. But unlike them, Loïs Mailou Jones included a background full of information. While her face and red shirt are the focal point, she wants you to see more. She expanded the idea of a self-portrait from just a painting of herself to a painting about her life. Let's see what she is trying to tell us.

Explore

Loïs Mailou Jones was an influential artist from Boston. She celebrated cultural emblems of African heritage in much of her work to show what was important to her. We'll explore:

- How did Jones use the painting to talk about her life?
- How did she design the painting and place forms in it artistically?

Composition and Design

The artist's figure is the main focus of the painting. With her brightly colored shirt and her direct gaze, she firmly holds our attention.

She positioned herself on the right to leave room on the rest of the canvas. While self-portraits are often for practice or experimentation, Jones wanted to tell us about her life as an African American artist, specifically her interest in African culture and her pride in her own work. The two figures in the background are African figurines. Other items honor her time in Paris, where she had lived and studied a few years earlier. Around her neck hangs a medallion that appears to say PARIS. Behind her she shows us one of her earlier works, *Les Pommes Vertes* (1937). In that painting, one of her favorites, a basket of green apples sits on a chair draped with a cloth.

Although the area behind Jones clearly shows objects, it's hard to figure out how the space in her studio could have resulted in the scale and angles shown. Jones seems to have stretched the bounds of realism to incorporate these objects into her design.

You might have noticed in the picture caption that Jones painted her self-portrait using casein, not oil paint. *Casein paints* are made from milk protein and they mix with water, unlike oil paints. Though used less than oils, they have a long history in art and are still available today.

Adding It Up

Often, self-portraits and portraits only show us the person they represent. This painting adds information about the artist's life by including objects and art that have cultural and personal meaning. The artist thought it was important for us to know more about her.

About Loïs Mailou Jones

Making art was an important part of Loïs Mailou Jones's childhood. Born in Boston, Massachusetts, in 1905, she remembered drawing at age three and being fascinated by color. Her mother was a beautician and hatmaker, and her father was the first Black graduate of Boston's Suffolk Law School. Her parents encouraged her creativity, sense of individuality, ambition, and commitment to her art. She spent summers on Martha's Vineyard, where the contrast between the island's brilliant beauty and Boston's gray cityscape inspired her to paint. There, she made lasting connections with Black intellectual and artistic elites, such as sculptor Meta Warrick Fuller, who had studied with Auguste Rodin in Paris and who encouraged Jones to train in Paris as well.

First, however, Jones studied art at a vocational high school and won a scholarship to Boston's School of the Museum of Fine Arts, where she excelled. Thinking she needed to pursue a practical career, she studied design and created bold, brilliantly colored textile patterns. Though she was successful, she wanted to be credited for her work, and set a goal to become a major artist. She added a concentration in portraiture to her studies, and focused on portraits throughout her life.

She was the museum school's first Black graduate and wanted to teach there, but she was rejected because she was African American. She first taught art and chaired the art department at the Palmer Memorial Institute in North Carolina and then was asked to join the art faculty at Howard University. At Howard she fought for promotions and pay equal to her male peers.

In 1937 Jones took a leave from teaching and won a scholarship to study in Paris. The city gave Jones glorious freedom from racism, and her painting flourished. She lived in a skylit studio with a view of the Eiffel Tower. Working with fervor, she produced more than 40 works over nine months. She painted in several styles. Inspired by Impressionist art, she used loose brushstrokes and a palette knife to give immediacy and texture to her paintings. She also worked in a stylized fashion, incorporating African artworks into her paintings and filling them with vibrant color. Like Laura Wheeler Waring, she celebrated Black culture in her portraits, whether her subjects were working class or the elite. Painting in Paris "gave me strength to realize my talent and that I really had the ability to succeed," she said.

Jones knew that her return to the United States would limit her freedom. When she tried to place her works in US galleries, she was rejected because of the color of her skin. In 1941 she asked a White friend to deliver a landscape to a competition at the Corcoran Gallery of Art in Washington, DC, where it not only was accepted but also won a prize. She insisted on receiving the prize by mail so that her identity would remain concealed. More than 50 years later, at the opening of its 1994 show dedicated to Jones's work, the museum officially apologized to her.

Jones's confidence helped her deal with the cruelty of discrimination. "I never let it affect me to the place where I became hateful, where I was not going to go on," she said. "I lived above it. I knew I was good. I kept saying to myself, 'I am going to make it on my strength as a painter.'"

Jones created opportunities for other Black artists to develop their talents. In the converted attic of her Washington, DC, home, she cofounded the Little Paris Studio, named in fond reference to her time in that city. Studio members met for weekly lessons and critiques and showed their paintings at a yearly exhibition. She also offered Saturday art classes for children.

Jones's many awards include being honored by President Jimmy Carter for her artistic achievements. Her works are in the permanent collections of major museums.

When she was in her 40s, Jones married a respected Haitian painter, Louis Vergniaud Pierre-Noël, and visits to Haiti highly influenced her style and color palette. She continued to focus on her art and had no children.

In her self-portrait, standing in front of her canvas, she looks directly at the viewer, confident, claiming her place as an artist, challenging the viewer to acknowledge her accomplishments.

Loïs Mailou Jones died at her Washington, DC, home in 1998.

Activity 8: Explore Edge Contrast

Areas of a drawing or painting that have hard edges will stand out more than blended, soft edges. In Loïs Mailou Jones's self-portrait, notice that color and value transitions on her face blend into each other—they have soft edges. In contrast, her hair has hard edges around it. Where else do you find hard and soft edges in her painting?

You'll Need

Pencil and eraser
Paper
Ruler
Small cloth scrap or paper towel

1. With your pencil and ruler, make three squares that measure about an inch on each side with about an inch between them.
2. Fill in the first square, staying inside the outlines and making crisp edges.
3. Fill in the middle square the same way, then smudge its edges for a few seconds with the cloth scrap or paper towel. NOTE: Some pencils are softer than others. A soft pencil will smudge more than a hard one.
4. Fill in the third square, and smudge its edges for about 20 seconds.
5. Which square stands out most against the white paper? Think how you might use hard and soft edges in a drawing or painting.

María Izquierdo, *Mi Tía, un Amiguito y Yo (My Aunt, a Little Friend, and Me)*, 1941. Oil on canvas, 54⅓ × 34¼ in. (138 × 87 cm). Colección Andrés Blaisten, México. Image copyright © Dr. Alberto Carmona Posadas. Photo credit: Museo Blaisten.

CHAPTER 19

María Izquierdo

Arrive

In this painting, staged like an old family photograph, the artist in her yellow dress and her aunt and friend stand stiffly, facing forward and barely smiling. The artist was not trying to copy a photograph. Instead, Izquierdo's imaginative, exuberant painting takes the idea of a photograph and blows it up to an almost life-size celebration of memory and imagination.

Explore

Let's look more closely at how María Izquierdo used the idea of a formal group photograph to inspire an imaginative painting that feels fun and serious at the same time. Perhaps she found an old photograph and used it for inspiration, but perhaps not. Mostly, Izquierdo worked from her imagination. Questions we'll explore are:

- How did Izquierdo use a grid for organization?
- How did Izquierdo create visual rhythm, like music that you can see?
- What are two ways she made herself the focus of the painting?

Composition

The flat, organized quality of this painting comes from a simple three-by-three grid. To see this, measure and trace lines dividing the painting horizontally and vertically into thirds, like a tic-tac-toe game. The line between the middle and lower third neatly divides the background and foreground, while the line between the middle and upper third crosses the gap between the aunt's sleeves and her gloves. Izquierdo placed each figure in a segment of the grid, allotting them each a measured space and deliberately placing herself in the center to draw our attention.

Covering up the umbrella makes the painting look unbalanced, demonstrating how the grid controls the design. Izquierdo needed something in that lower left grid space, making the umbrella a charming fourth character in her setup.

Lights and Darks

Izquierdo used value contrast to call attention to the children, painting the top half of the painting much darker than the bottom half. She also playfully used value contrast throughout the image. Dark strokes contrast against lighter areas in the background and clothing. In lines and curves that are large, small, long, and short, they add liveliness and rhythm and break up the grid's rigidity.

Color

Izquierdo's warm, vibrant colors work with the value contrasts to highlight the foreground and especially the children. Look at the skin's gold hues, the reddish-violet umbrella, the aunt's warm dark-orange skirt, and the boy's bright red belt and shoes. And the artist? She wears a pale and buttery dress, the lightest and brightest color in the painting, to make sure we focus on her.

Adding It Up

This painting is an imaginative and modern take on a nostalgic glimpse into old times and childhood. Whether the painting is based on a real photo or not, it shows us the artist's connection to her young self and people that were important to her.

About María Izquierdo

Born in 1902 in San Juan de los Lagos, Mexico, María Izquierdo did not grow up drawing, painting, or visiting museums. The art she knew came from traditions in music, dance, religion, story, and decoration. Unlike some other artists who chose an artistic life rather than marriage or family, Izquierdo was only 14 when her grandparents arranged for her to marry.

When she, her husband, and their three children moved to Mexico City, Izquierdo became fascinated and inspired by the city's vibrant art scene. She began painting at home, then studied at the city's premier arts institute, the Escuela Nacional de Bellas Artes. She separated from her husband and lived with the artist Rufino Tamayo, a painter of colorful, often surrealistic abstracted images, who influenced her work. At the art school, her portraits and still lifes gained attention from prominent artists like muralist Diego Rivera, who had left his partner Angelina Beloff in France and married artist Frida Kahlo when he returned to Mexico.

When Diego Rivera toured the school, he found just three paintings worthy of attention. They were all by Izquierdo. Other painters were jealous and treated her unkindly. She soon left the school. "The path that the woman who paints must travel is terribly hard!"

she wrote. Even a mural commission she received was taken away from her when it was learned she planned to feature women.

Izquierdo's bright colors, thick, curving lines, and dramatic subjects portray a world full of mystery and emotion. Her portraits of women, including circus performers, show strength and beauty. She reached deep into her own emotions and experiences to paint, creating works referencing traditional Mexican culture. She did not use models or set up objects to portray in her still lifes. She painted from memory, not from anything in front of her.

She wrote of her intuitive approach, "You do not paint with your hands: the painting should be born in your soul, pass through your brain, and then your emotions must spill it onto a canvas, panel, or wall."

In 1930 Izquierdo traveled to New York, where her work was part of a group exhibition at the Metropolitan Museum of Art. She also showed 14 paintings at the Art Center in New York, becoming the first Mexican woman to have a solo show in the United States.

Izquierdo's health affected her work. After a stroke paralyzed the right side of her body, including the hand she used to hold her paintbrush, she trained herself to paint using her left hand. Her health continued to suffer, and she died in 1955 of another stroke.

Amelia Peláez, *Marpacífico (Hibiscus)*, 1943. Oil on canvas, 45½ × 35 in. (115.6 × 88.9 cm). OAS AMA / Art Museum of the Americas Collection, gift of IBM. © Amelia Peláez Foundation. Photo credit: Collection OAS AMA / Art Museum of the Americas.

CHAPTER 20

Amelia Peláez

Arrive

Bold orange and red hibiscus blossoms pop forward from big blue and brown shapes behind them. This 1943 painting of a vase of flowers differs from Rachel Ruysch's 1716 bouquet in every way. Yet both dramatically change a common subject into something special. As tall as an eight-year-old and just as lively, this painting feels free, cheerful, and fun.

Explore

The vase of flowers takes up three-fourths of *Marpacífico's* 45-inch height. Behind it, we might be looking at some furniture, and behind that are black, blue, and brown shapes that are hard to identify. Above, Peláez

playfully renders the fancy trim around the blue ceiling in a style that is almost like doodling. It's easy to imagine the artist having fun making this still life. Let's explore:

- What are the building blocks that make the painting fun and cheerful?
- How does the design keep the painting grounded?

Line, Shape, and Color

Although this is a painting, it looks like a drawing that was filled in with color, like a page in a coloring book. Peláez "wrote" black lines all over the canvas, including squiggles, Xs, and zigzags. She formed big shapes and filled them with patterns. She drew the lines and shapes with a confident and free hand. The flower shapes themselves are zany simplifications of a real hibiscus's bell-shaped, five-petal blossoms.

Peláez combined rich color with her exuberant line drawing. She used white, gray, brown, and blue in the background. These dark, cool colors give those orange and white blossoms maximum popping power. The value and hue really contrast to grab your attention. White and black are opposites in value, and orange and blue are opposites on the color wheel. (See the appendix, pp. 175–176.)

Composition and Design

Though the drawing seems free and spontaneous, the composition, as with Tarsila's painting, uses a design based on balanced asymmetry. If you folded *Marpacífico* in half, you'd see that each side looks similar. The arc of the abstract ceiling design directs our eyes right to the blossoms bursting from the middle.

Adding It Up

Peláez emphasized three artistic building blocks in this painting: line, shape, and color. Freely drawn lines and bright complementary colors energize the balanced design. *Marpacífico* shows us that art can be playful and still be great art.

About Amelia Peláez

Born in 1896 just before Cuba gained political independence from Spain, Amelia Peláez was a Cuban painter and ceramicist whose energetic black lines and vibrant colors, whether on canvas or on clay, exude warmth and liveliness.

Peláez's uncle was a poet, and her father was a doctor who moved his family from a small town to Havana when Peláez was 16. She attended the Academia San Alejandro, which she felt prepared her for her studies in the United States and Europe. Her early works were brushstroke-heavy landscapes of rural scenes and gentle, fluid landscapes and still lifes.

After a 1924 solo show in Havana, Peláez broadened her artistic education at New York's Art Students League, and spent seven years in Europe, studying at several academies, including the École du Louvre. Her time in Paris enabled her to meld modern European influences with her Cuban culture.

At Cubist painter Fernand Léger's newly founded Académie Moderne in Paris, she studied design and color theory with Alexandra Exter, a theater designer and painter of energetic, brilliantly colored abstract works. Exter had a major influence on Peláez's work and considered her among the most talented of all her students.

In 1933 Peláez exhibited 38 pictures in a solo show at Paris's Galerie Zak, which represented Latin American and Polish artists. The next year, she returned to Havana. In the garden of her family home, decorated by tall columns and intricate ironwork that became recurring design elements, Peláez set up a studio and became active in the Cuban modernist movement.

"The artist, as I see it," she said, "is nothing more than a hardworking craftsman who has purified and refined his or her trade, which requires daily, constant labor, an effort that must unfold on a daily basis throughout life, from the beginning to the end."

Marpacífico and 10 other Peláez works, including watercolors, pencil drawings, and oils, were featured in a 1944 exhibit of 13 Cuban modernist painters at New York's Museum of Modern Art. Peláez was the only woman included, and the MOMA *Bulletin* praised her works' "intricacy" and "brilliance of color."

Of the Cuban modernist trend, the *Bulletin* noted, "It has something of the brashness, but even more the virtues of youth—courage, freshness, vitality, and a healthy disrespect for its elders in a country which is very old in tradition and very new in independence." A 1942 Peláez watercolor, *Balcony*, graced the catalog's cover.

Peláez had several solo shows, won prizes at four of Cuba's National Salons, was recognized by the Guggenheim International Award committee, and exhibited internationally. She created two massive ceramic murals in Havana. One was a dynamic pattern in blue, yellow, and burnt sienna stretching across one side of the city's

Tribunal de Cuentas; the other, a playful composition in shades of blue along the Habana Hilton hotel's facade. Cuban art critic and curator José Gómez Sicre, who organized the MOMA exhibition, said in 1957 that Amelia Peláez's art was "among the most outstanding painting Cuba has so far produced."

Amelia Peláez died in Havana in 1968.

Activity 9: Explore Color Contrast

The strong color contrasts in Amelia Peláez's painting make it exciting and fun to look at. Have some fun playing with color contrasts in this activity.

You'll Need

Pencil and eraser
Paper
Ruler
Colored pencils, crayons, or markers

1. With your pencil and ruler, lightly draw a 3-by-4-inch rectangle.
2. Inside it, make a design of squiggles that make lots of enclosed shapes.
3. Pick three colors that are near each other on the color wheel. (See the appendix, p. 176.) Fill in the design with those colors.
4. Make a new rectangle and a new squiggle design and fill it with three colors that are far apart on the color wheel.
5. Try it a third time with a bright color and two dull ones.
6. Look over your work. Think about how the different color schemes affect the drawing's mood and focus. How might you use color contrast in a drawing or painting?

Maria Leontina, *Natureza Morta (Still Life)*, 1952. Oil
on canvas, 28¾ × 39⅜ in. (73 × 100 cm). National
Museum of Fine Arts Collection / Brazilian Institute
of Museums / Ministry of Tourism, authorization
number 06/2021. Image copyright © Alexandre
Franco Dacosta. Photo credit: Museu Nacional
de Belas Artes. Photographer: Jaime Acioli.

Maria Leontina

Arrive

On your first look at this mid-20th-century painting, you might see a flat design of fruit and dishes against an irregular patchwork. Gaze longer and the painting begins to look less flat. The objects appear closer on the left than on the right, and the patchwork behind the pink glasses seems to include a distant doorway. Let's look at how Maria Leontina played with perception, creating a painting that looks flat and deep at the same time.

Explore

Abstract art can simplify familiar objects and ask us to look at them in new ways. Often, abstract artists present an idea for us to think about. Here, Leontina asks us to consider how the way we see pattern interacts with the way we see space. She offers the example of fruit and dishes on a table in a room. Let's explore:

- How did Leontina make the painting look flat?
- How did she make the painting have depth?

Reading the Painting

Let's look first at the objects in this painting. The fruit stand, fruit, knife, and glasses spread across from left to right. They have no details and aren't painted to show that they are three-dimensional—they could easily be a collage of paper. The way they are painted makes them look flat, but their sizes and positions and the way they are layered tell us we're looking into a three-dimensional space: The fruit dish is closest to us, then the knife, then the line of fruit. We can tell what is in front of an object and what is behind it.

The background and setting are also painted in a flat style. At first, seeing the same patchwork shapes and colors everywhere makes it hard to separate forms from one another. In fact, Leontina varied the patchwork throughout the setting. On the tabletop and tablecloth the patches are diagonal, on the walls they are vertical, and on the floor they are horizontal.

This very modern still life is composed using the classical composition idea of placing the focal point, the fruit dish, where the thirds intersect: the dish's pedestal is on the vertical one-third line, and its top is at the horizontal two-thirds line.

Color Notes

While shapes and pattern drive this painting, the design gets a boost from color and light. To enhance the focal point, Leontina painted the fruit dish bright white so it stands out from everything else. She painted the fruits in strong colors—black, pink, yellow, and green—so they would stand out too. She balanced the black fruit on the left with the black glass on the right. These objects contrast with the quiet, subdued shades of red, yellow, and blue on the rest of the canvas.

Adding It Up

Have you ever tried to look at both sides of an argument before you pick a side? This painting is like that. On the one hand, Leontina painted every form to look flat. On the other hand, she created depth through size, layering, position, and color. So is the painting meant to look flat or not? Perhaps the artist's answer is that we don't always have to choose sides. This still life is flat, and it is not.

About Maria Leontina

Maria Leontina created abstract artworks with geometric shapes that remade ordinary scenes into something extraordinary. For her, "to paint is to play with enigmas," one critic wrote. He praised her paintings' "poetic" language, noting that their shapes seem to almost speak to each other, and likened her work to that of Paul Klee and Joan Miró.

Born in São Paulo, Brazil, in 1917, Maria Leontina began studying drawing and painting at age 21. One of her influential teachers, Lasar Segall, created modern, expressive works bursting with bright color that combined realistic figures with abstracted yet recognizable elements.

Leontina and her husband, the painter Milton Dacosta, studied in Paris for two years on a grant from the French government. Both were attracted to geometric abstraction, and Leontina also studied printmaking with a noted German artist.

Interested in exploring her subjects in different ways, Leontina often created her works in series. She used flat planes of color, meticulously constructing her puzzle-like pieces in colors that were sometimes saturated, other times muted. She created intricate etchings with interwoven, fluid lines. "I was an expressionist, like almost all artists at that time," she said.

Leontina had her first solo show when she was 33, and she exhibited at the Venice Biennale. She won a prize in a juried exhibit of 19 painters in 1947, and she and Tarsila do Amaral each won prizes for their paintings at the Bienal de São Paulo in 1951, which aimed to showcase Brazil's modern art on an international level. In 1960 Leontina's painting *Les Episodes III* won the Guggenheim Foundation's National Award for Brazil.

Leontina also created a ceramic panel for the massive, newly built Copan Building, a landmark wave-like structure in São Paulo. She wrote art reviews and taught art at a psychiatric hospital.

Drawing remained fundamental to her art practice. "I draw a lot," Leontina wrote. "I like to elaborate the drawing inside me, so that it appears spontaneous. The drawing is very useful, always."

Maria Leontina died in Rio de Janeiro in 1984.

Pan Yuliang, *Nude* (a.k.a. *Seated Nude*), 1953. Oil on canvas, 13 × 18¼ in. (33.0 × 46.4 cm). Musée Cernuschi, Paris, France (inv. 38967-6). *Droits réservés*. Photo credit: © RMN-Grand Palais / Art Resource, NY.

CHAPTER 22

Pan Yuliang

Arrive

In this small painting, fine lines trace the folded shapes formed by a woman's body. Though the subject is nude, this painting is about privacy as well as exposure. The model's folded pose and dropped head protect her identity. With her face hidden, she becomes an anonymous symbol of the grace and beauty of the human form.

Explore

Student artists learn to draw and paint people by sketching from a live nude model. Throughout art history, artists have portrayed nudes to illustrate myths and allegories, to celebrate the beauty of the human body, to protest mistreatment of women, and at other times simply to shock. In this example, Pan Yuliang carefully protects her model while emphasizing her grace. Let's explore:

- What are contour lines, and how did Pan Yuliang use them to convey her idea?
- How does the lack of identity and background affect the way we see this painting?

Line, Shape, and Form

Let's take a closer look. The body is a closed shape completely separate from the background. From the designs at the bottom we can tell that the model is on a cushion or blanket. We have no other information about where she's sitting, or how big or deep the space is.

Lines drawn to describe shapes are called *contour lines*. Pan's contour lines separate the body from the background and show its arrangement in space. She hid parts of the head and left arm behind other body parts, and *foreshortened* the foot, showing that it's turned toward us.

Pan painted the model's body in a flat, golden color that separates it from the lighter background. The model's shape is like an arch or a triangle with rounded corners and is grounded, balanced, and graceful. Notice other triangles that make up her shape. You can even see a spiral of triangles inside one another, beginning with the triangle formed by her bent legs.

Imaginative Interpretations

Let's go back to the big picture. The concealing pose, absence of face, vague background, and earthy colors add up to an abstract composition that focuses on shape. This is very different from a portrait, whose goal is to celebrate identity. This painting is so abstract the woman's shape might bring to mind other objects with similar shapes that are different in scale. The shape is like mountains and foothills, a pile of rocks on a beach, or even a tiny snail with a spiral shell. What do you see in it?

Adding It Up

Nude uses contour lines to capture the abstract beauty of the human shape. Pan Yuliang lets us think about what art can reveal and what it can hide through what she included and what she left out.

About Pan Yuliang

Pan Yuliang's life spanned two countries and two cultures, and she created her own artistic style out of those traditions. Born in 1895 in Yangzhou, China, a city near the Yangtze River, she lived half her life in China and half her life in Paris. Her father died before she was a year old, and her mother and older sister died when she was eight. In her teens her uncle sold her into a brothel, but she was able to leave when she married a customs official, Pan Zanhua, in 1912 and took her husband's family name, Pan.

Pan's husband taught her to write, and she began studying painting with a private instructor. In 1920 she was accepted into the Shanghai Art School, which was influenced by Western-style painting, especially French Impressionism, and was its first woman graduate.

Art instruction in China at the time was influenced by artists' experience with modern Japanese art, which incorporated European-style painting. Chinese artists began to study in Japan; then, back in China, art schools in Beijing and Nanjing started teaching methods of European-style representation. The Shanghai Art School pioneered art exhibitions and the practice of painting from live models, both clothed and nude.

Chinese artists began studying in France in the early 1900s. In 1922 Pan won a grant to study at the French-Chinese Institute in Lyon, France, and then attended two French national art schools; one was also in Lyon, and the other was the École des Beaux-Arts in Paris. In Paris she studied with French painter Lucien Simon, whose own work was lively and full of movement and who also taught Amrita Sher-Gil. Pan also studied sculpture at Rome's Accademia di Belle Arti, and her accomplishments were chronicled in Chinese newspapers.

Pan's work reflects the brilliant colors and immediacy of Impressionists such as Claude Monet and Pierre-Auguste Renoir. Said to be a bold, forthright woman, she created emotion-filled self-portraits in which she challenges the viewer, as well as landscapes and still lifes. Pan used traditional Chinese brush techniques in her expressive line paintings of nudes, which recall Henri Matisse's shapes and make up about half of Pan's 4,000 works.

Pan returned to Shanghai in 1928 and exhibited in her first solo show. She was prominent among women painters and chaired the Department of Western Art at Shanghai Art School, taught at New China Art School, and became a fine arts professor at Nanjing Central University. In 1937 she showed 170 works, including some nudes, in a solo exhibition. In August of that year, she went to Paris to attend the Paris Exposition Internationale des Arts et Techniques, which had the goal of uniting art and technology.

Pan was prevented from returning to China by World War II and China's Cultural Revolution. Later she attempted to go back but was told she would have to leave all of her artwork behind. She never returned to China.

In spring 1977, Paris's Musée Cernuschi held an exhibition of Pan's works along with three other Chinese woman artists. That same year, Pan Yuliang died in Paris, where she is buried in Montparnasse Cemetery, among many celebrated artists and writers.

Activity 10: Look for Abstract Shapes

In Pan Yuliang's painting, the figure's shape is similar to the shape of a landscape or rocks or even a snail. At the heart of most drawings and paintings are simple shapes that could become many different objects depending on how the artist develops them.

You'll Need

Pencil and eraser
Paper
Ruler or small index card

1. On three different pieces of paper, draw a 3-by-5-inch rectangle (or you can trace a small index card). Draw it so that a short side is on the bottom.
2. On the first page, add details that make the rectangle into a tall building. You can add extra shapes to the top and sides if you want to. What scenery will you add around it?
3. On the second page, add details that turn the rectangle into a carton of milk. Add some dishes or food around it to make a still life.
4. The third page is up to you. What will you turn this rectangle into? Some ideas: a window, a refrigerator, a swimming pool seen from above . . . What will you draw next?
5. Keep an eye out for basic shapes in the world around you: Where do you see rectangles, squares, triangles, circles, and ovals? Artists use these simple shapes to help them draw many objects. How can you use them in your next drawing?

Alma Woodsey Thomas, *Red Abstraction*, 1959. Oil on canvas, 40 × 27¾ in. (101.6 × 70.5 cm). Smithsonian American Art Museum, Washington, DC, gift of the artist (1978.40.2). Photo credit: Smithsonian American Art Museum, Washington, DC / Art Resource, NY.

CHAPTER 23

Alma Woodsey Thomas

Arrive

When you show up at *Red Abstraction*, you might feel a little lost. Maybe you wonder what you're supposed to see or how you're supposed to react. There's nothing you can name here—the painting is neither realistic nor representational—so take a few minutes and simply look around. Absorb the experience of this painting from the "color field" movement, in which painters brushed big fields of color across their abstract canvases.

Explore

Let's start exploring how to look at totally abstract paintings from the 20th century.

Most artists use paint to show you people, places, events, and things. In the 20th century artists started experimenting with the idea that paintings did not have to show you anything. They used pure color, shape, surface, and line to communicate ideas and concepts like joy, tension, excitement, peace, or love. Some abstract paintings, like Alma Thomas's *Red Abstraction*, were inspired by how something real made the artist feel— in this case, Thomas's garden. The idea of a garden of red flowers brings energy and growth to mind. Perhaps that's what Thomas started out trying to paint: not flowers, but the feeling of flowers.

Let's explore *Red Abstraction*:

- What are you "supposed" to see in this painting?
- How did Thomas's use of color and shape give the painting its energy?

Let the Painting Be

Take a little time to look at this painting. Start to notice how your eye travels around *Red Abstraction*. Give yourself permission to *not* know what it's about. Instead, let it be what it is. Then, start to notice places that interest you more than others.

Energy Sources

Although there's no "thing" in the painting, there's a feeling in it, a sense of energy. How do you paint energy? Thomas used the same tools every painter has, including color and shape.

Artists know that red always stands out. One source of energy Thomas used is the color itself, this particularly rich, warm shade of red. The second source is the way she used it, making it dominate the composition in a wild shape that seems to push outward as if it were expanding and trying to break free of the canvas. The red shape is irregular and unpredictable, constantly changing, its edges sometimes soft and smudgy and sometimes crisp. While the red seems to push out, the background—a negative shape—seems to be trying to hold it in.

There are colors other than red in the painting. The mysterious green and dark brown shapes at the top left create a focal point that attracts our attention. The background is filled with pale colors, and the red itself is not a flat field of color. These color variations appear unpredictably and imbue every inch of the canvas with interest.

Adding It Up

Energy is a main idea in Alma Thomas's color field painting *Red Abstraction*. The energy comes from the kind of red, its shape, and the way it pushes out against the edges. Had Alma Thomas painted her garden realistically, we could have named her flowers but we might not have understood the feeling they inspired.

About Alma Woodsey Thomas

Alma Woodsey Thomas was born in 1891 in Columbus, Georgia, the first of four girls in an African American family. Her grandfather built a school on his cotton plantation and instilled in his grandchildren a respect for education. He grilled them on spelling and kept them up to date on news and politics.

Thomas's mother went to Tuskegee Institute, became a dressmaker and designer, and was part of a women's club that periodically met at her home to study the classics and painting. Thomas remembered being fascinated by tubes of oil paint, but she dreamed of being an architect, not an artist.

Her father, a businessman, built a stately Victorian home in Columbus, and the family's home was surrounded by extensive flower gardens. Those gardens imprinted on Thomas's memory and are represented in her abstract paintings.

Columbus did not provide schooling for Black students past grade school, and its public library barred Black residents. In 1907 the Thomas family moved to Washington, DC.

Her high school art classes in Washington "were so exciting," she wrote, that they opened "a whole new door for me that extended into the future." She began teaching, then enrolled at Howard University, and was its first student to graduate with a fine arts degree. She studied sketching from live models, costume design, painting, and sculpture.

Thomas took a job as assistant director of drawing at the Cheyney Training School for Teachers in Pennsylvania, where portrait artist Laura Wheeler Waring was on faculty. Waring would later paint Thomas's portrait.

Back in Washington, DC, Thomas began teaching art at a junior high and devoted herself to expanding her students' interest in and access to art. She created the city's first public school art gallery and organized lectures and gallery shows featuring Black artists.

While still teaching, she spent 10 years studying painting at American University. She also studied at Columbia University's Teachers College and learned marionette-making from puppeteer Tony Sarg, who created the balloons for the first Macy's Thanksgiving Day parades.

After her 38-year teaching career, Thomas concentrated on her own painting. She was a member of Loïs Mailou Jones's Little Paris Studio and showed three of her paintings at the group's first exhibition in 1951. At age 67 she had her first solo show at American University.

For Thomas, color was everything. Encouraged by Jones to work more abstractly, she moved from more realistic painting to creating exuberant, brilliantly colored patterns. The 1969 moon landing inspired a series of paintings about space, including *Snoopy Sees a Sunrise*, which is in the Smithsonian's National Air and Space Museum. She wanted not to copy nature but to create the joyful feeling that nature gave her. Inspired by patterns made by the light through the holly tree outside her garden, she used small rectangular blocks of color to create mosaiclike paintings. She called those paintings "Alma's Stripes."

"I've never bothered painting the ugly things in life . . . no," she said. "I wanted something beautiful that you could sit down and look at."

Three Thomas paintings have been displayed at the White House. President and Mrs. Obama chose a concentric-circle, rainbow-colored painting, *Resurrection*

(1966), the first by a Black woman artist to be added to the White House Collection. Thomas also was the first Black woman artist to have a solo show at the Whitney Museum of American Art. Yet Black artists, she felt, draw on their experiences like any other artist. "In my opinion," she wrote, "Black art is a misnomer." Traditional African art is "profound" and has had a great influence on modern art, she wrote, yet nonrepresentational art doesn't present as necessarily Black or White. She wanted her work to bring joy to herself and others. "Through color I have sought to concentrate on beauty and happiness in my painting," she wrote, "rather than on man's inhumanity to man."

Alma Thomas died in 1978 in Washington, DC.

Joan Mitchell, *Marlin*, 1960. Oil on canvas, 95 × 71 in. (241.3 × 180.3 cm). Smithsonian American Art Museum, Washington, DC, gift of S. C. Johnson & Son Inc. © Estate of Joan Mitchell. Photo credit: Smithsonian American Art Museum, Washington, DC / Art Resource, NY.

CHAPTER 24

Joan Mitchell

Arrive

Our last painting is a big one. And it's splashy.

As with Alma Thomas's painting, spend time just sitting with Joan Mitchell's work. Make note of your perceptions and any feelings or ideas it brings to mind.

Let's describe it. Again—it's huge! Against a warm gray background, color marks whirl and whip. Dark colors pool in the middle, and as we sink to the bottom, shapes seem to emerge. As we rise, the colors come apart, disintegrating into splashes of lines. There's a sense of slowness near the bottom and speed at the top. The painting is called *Marlin*—a deep sea fish of great size, speed, and strength.

Explore

Let's take a closer look. *Marlin* is an example of Abstract Expressionism, where the painter uses color, shapes, surface, and lines without being representational. The point is not to show you something specific. You might keep looking at *Marlin*, trying to find something in it that you recognize, even though the painting is completely abstract. Do you find yourself thinking you almost see a . . . and a . . . ? Is it there? Or not?

Joan Mitchell was famous for large abstract paintings made of bold strokes of color. Let's explore:

- Why is this painting so big?
- How does Mitchell's painting style play with our eyes?

Size

The size of *Marlin* is part of its message. Imagine that you are able to see it in a museum, almost 6 feet wide and 8 feet tall. The size gives it power and makes it loud and unforgettable.

That said, shown here at about the size of a postcard, *Marlin* is still lively and full of movement. Let's look more closely at Mitchell's style. She piled on the paint in the lower half using thick strokes with a big brush or other tool. There's nothing shy about these masses of blue, brown, and white. Moving up higher, when she must have been on a ladder, you can see the arcs of her brushstrokes showing the sweep of her arm. Her technique and style make you think the artist was adventurous and fearless.

Adding It Up

Joan Mitchell's *Marlin* is full of movement and power, and if it had a voice it would be loud. These qualities are fueled by Mitchell's painting style and *Marlin*'s great size. Her style is unique in managing to be completely abstract while also hinting at things we might recognize. Because it's an abstract painting, if you're not sure what to think at first, be patient and let the painting talk to you—or maybe shout, in the case of *Marlin*.

About Joan Mitchell

Born in Chicago in 1925, Joan Mitchell grew up in a large apartment overlooking Lake Michigan. She first felt drawn to art as a young child, when she experienced "the clouds and the sky and the wind" from her balcony.

Mitchell had an art-filled childhood. Her mother edited *Poetry* magazine, and her father was a prominent dermatologist who drew and painted. The poets Robert Frost and Edna St. Vincent Millay came for dinner at her home. On visits to the Art Institute of Chicago, she was especially impressed by the art of Vincent van Gogh.

Mitchell sketched and painted, beginning at age six or seven, and wrote poetry. She was published in *Poetry* magazine when she was 10. Her poem, "Autumn," is filled with painterly images: "rusty leaves," "blue haze," and "sun-tanned stalks," and also with sadness at the death of the growing season and the chilly winter to come.

Though her father insisted Mitchell choose between writing and painting so that she could focus her talent and become successful, poetry remained a lifelong passion. She thought of her paintings as poetic expressions. "My paintings repeat a feeling about Lake Michigan, or water, or fields. . . . It's more like a poem, and that's what I want to paint."

Mitchell intensely worked on her painting at a summer art colony and later enrolled at the Art Institute of Chicago. She painted in Mexico and Paris before moving into a New York studio.

In New York Mitchell exhibited at the groundbreaking 1951 9th Street Art Exhibition of Paintings and Sculpture and had her first solo show the next year, but she had moments when she questioned her ability.

"When I was discouraged I wondered if really women couldn't paint," she told an interviewer, "the way all the men said they [the women] couldn't paint."

During her career, her brilliantly colored work developed from expressive representational landscapes and portraits to the energy-filled abstract works for which she became famous. She likened her exhilaration while painting to "riding a bike with no hands."

Mitchell moved to Paris in 1959 and later settled in the French countryside, in the same village where Claude Monet once spent summers and painted. For 20 years she lived with the abstract painter Jean-Paul Riopelle.

Mitchell painted her large-scale works in a stone building on her property, often working at night while listening to music. While her paintings' energy might make it seem as if she painted quickly, Mitchell worked deliberately, assessing each brushstroke and taking care to step back and view her work from a distance.

"She has led the kind of thoroughgoing artistic life that anyone might dream of, if they dream of being an artist," said art critic and friend Bill Berkson. "In her twenties, she went straight to the mark: she quickly became the painter she clearly meant to be."

Joan Mitchell died of cancer in 1992 in France.

Appendix

Value Scale

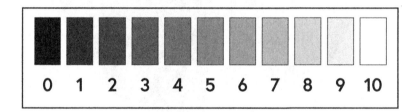

Color Wheel

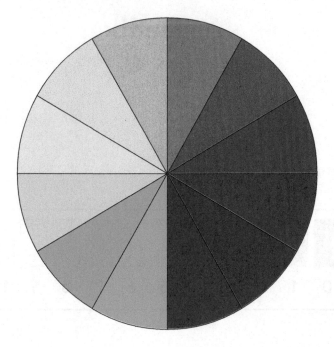

Notes

1. Lavinia Fontana

"This excellent Painter": Flavia Frigeri, *Women Artists* (London: Thames & Hudson, 2019), 10.

"In painting there are those who know": Katherine A. McIver, "Lavinia Fontana's 'Self-Portrait Making Music,'" *Woman's Art Journal* 19, no. 1 (Spring–Summer 1998): 7, via JSTOR, https://www.jstor.org/stable/1358647.

2. Artemisia Gentileschi

"A woman's name": Keith Christiansen and Judith W. Mann, *Orazio and Artemisia Gentileschi* (New York: Metropolitan Museum of Art, 2001), 271.

"I will show": Christiansen and Mann, 271.

5. Rosa Bonheur

"I wed art": Anna Klumpke, *Rosa Bonheur: The Artist's (Auto)biography* (Ann Arbor: University of Michigan Press, 1977), xviii.

"Had I been a man": Elaine Sciolino, "The Redemption of Rosa Bonheur," *Smithsonian*, November 2020, 73.

"divine marriage of two souls": Sciolino, 73.

6. Berthe Morisot

"so-called art": Christoph Heinrich, *Monet* (Los Angeles: Taschen, 2000), 45.

"I don't think there has ever been": Anne Higonnet, *Berthe Morisot* (Berkeley: University of California Press, 1995), 203.

"Work is the sole purpose": Denis Rouart, ed., *Berthe Morisot: The Correspondence with Her Family and Friends Manet, Puvis de Chavannes, Degas, Monet, Renoir and Mallarme*, trans. Betty W. Hubbard (Mt. Kisco, NY: Moyer Bell, 1987), 66.

7. Mary Cassatt

"I am not willing to admit": Charlotte Streifer Rubinstein, *American Women Artists: From Early Indian Times to the Present* (Boston: G. K. Hall, 1982), 135.

8. Cecilia Beaux

"not only the greatest living woman painter": "Ernesta," Metropolitan Museum of Art, accessed July 8, 2021, https://www.metmuseum.org/art/collection/search/10126.

"success is sexless": "Cecilia Beaux Dies: A Portrait Artist," *New York Times*, September 18, 1942.

9. Lluïsa Vidal

"She paints so well": Marcy Rudo, "Painted Like a Man, Disappeared Like a Woman: Luisa Vidal, the Daughter Of Modernism," OTI Online, Summer 1998, https://www.ontheissuesmagazine.com/1998summer/su98_Rudo.php.

10. Angel De Cora

"ideal": Angel De Cora, "Angel De Cora (Winnebago)," in *Recovering Native American Writings in the Boarding School Press*, ed. Jacqueline Emery (Lincoln: University of Nebraska Press, 2017), 249, via JSTOR, https://www.jstor.org/stable/j.ctt1w76tq5.

"I am Indian": L. M. Waggoner, *Fire Light: The Life of Angel De Cora, Winnebago Artist* (Norman: University of Oklahoma Press, 2008), 78.

"I now feel that Miss de Cora": Waggoner, 79.

11. Suzanne Valadon

"If I were to purchase something here": Catherine Hewitt, *Renoir's Dancer: The Secret Life of Suzanne Valadon* (New York: St. Martin's Press, 2017), 327.

12. Paula Modersohn-Becker

"Whenever I talk with somebody": Diane Radycki, *Paula Modersohn-Becker: The First Modern Woman Artist* (New Haven, CT: Yale University Press, 2013), 57.

"I am savouring my life": Paula Modersohn-Becker, *Paula Modersohn-Becker: The Letters and Journals*, ed. Günter Busch, Liselotte von Reinken, and Arthur S. Wensinger (Evanston, IL: Northwestern University Press, 1998), 108.

"Your two letters": Modersohn-Becker, 159.

14. Tarsila do Amaral

"the painter of my country": Aliza Edelman, "Tarsila do Amaral: The Mother of Brazilian Modernism," *Apollo Magazine*, February 13, 2018, https://www.apollo-magazine.com/tarsila-do-amaral-the-mother-of-brazilian-modernism/.

"I found in Minas": "Biography," Tarsila Site Oficial, accessed July 9, 2021, http://tarsiladoamaral.com.br/en/biography/.

16. Amrita Sher-Gil

"It seems that I never began painting": Usha Kakkar, "Amrita Shergill the Pioneer Artist," *Punjab Monitor*, April

7, 2013, http://www.punjabmonitor.com/2013/04 /amrita-shergill-pioneer-artist.html.

"Towards the end of 1933": Saloni Mathur, "A Retake of Sher-Gil's *Self-Portrait as Tahitian,*" *Critical Inquiry* 37, no. 3 (Spring 2011): 534, via JSTOR, https://www.jstor .org/stable/10.1086/659356.

"modern art has led me": N. Iqbal Singh, "Amrita Sher-Gil," *India International Centre Quarterly* 2, no. 3 (July 1975): 213, via JSTOR, https://www.jstor.org/stable /23001838.

"to interpret the life": Singh, 210.

17. Yuki Ogura

"I have a vivid memory": Nanako Yamada, "The Figure Paintings of Ogura Yuki: The Merging of East and West," *Woman's Art Journal* 25, no. 2 (Autumn 2004– Winter 2005): 3.

"Something Bright, Warm, and Pleasant": Yamada, 6.

18. Loïs Mailou Jones

"gave me strength to realize": Charles H. Rowell, "An Interview with Loïs Mailou Jones," *Callaloo*, no. 39 (Spring 1989): 357–378, via JSTOR, https://www.jstor.org /stable/2931576.

"I never let it affect me": Betty LaDuke, "Lois Mailou Jones: The Grande Dame of African-American Art," *Woman's Art Journal* 8, no. 2 (Autumn 1987–Winter 1988): 29, via JSTOR, https://www.jstor.org/stable /1358163.

19. María Izquierdo

"The path that the woman": Nancy Deffebach, *María Izquierdo and Frida Kahlo: Challenging Visions in Modern Mexican Art* (Austin: University of Texas Press, 2016), 172.

"You do not paint with your hands": Deffebach, 183.

20. Amelia Peláez

"The artist, as I see it": Amelia Peláez, interview by José Seoane Gallo, 1963–1967, in *José Seoane Gallo, Palmas Reales en el Sena* (Havana: Editorial Letras Cubanas, 1987), 161, quoted in René Morales, "The Craft of Memory," Pérez Art Museum Miami, accessed July 12, 2021, https://www.pamm.org/sites/default /files/amelia_pelaez_craft_final_final_0.pdf, 8.

"intricacy" and "brilliance": Alfred H. Barr Jr., "Modern Cuban Painters," *Bulletin of the Museum of Modern Art* 11, no. 5 (April 1944): 3, via JSTOR, https://www.jstor .org/stable/4058172.

"It has something of the brashness": Barr, 2.

"among the most outstanding painting": "Amelia Peláez b.1896, d.1968 Cuba," Art Museum of the Americas, accessed July 12, 2021, http://www.oas.org/arts oftheamericas/amelia-pelaez.

21. Maria Leontina

"to paint is to play with enigmas": Ferreira Gullar, "Maria Leontina," *Prêmio Leirner de Arte Contemporâneo: Giselda Leiner, María Leontina, Tomie Ohtake, Hércules Barsotti, Willys de Castro* (São Paulo: Galeria de Arte das Folhas, 1959), digitized by Documents of Latin American and Latino Art, International Center for the Arts of the Americas at the Museum of Fine Arts, Houston, https://icaa.mfah.org/s/en/item /1324995#?c=&m=&s=&cv=&xywh=-2001%2C -284%2C6551%2C3666.

"I was an expressionist": "Maria Leontina," Enciclopédia Itaú Cultural, last modified January 6, 2021, http://enciclopedia.itaucultural.org.br/pessoa8721 /maria-leontina.

"I draw a lot": "Maria Leontina," *Enciclopédia Itaú Cultural.*

23. Alma Woodsey Thomas

"were so exciting": Alma Thomas papers, circa 1894– 2001, series 3 (Notes and Writings), box 2, folder 7 (Autobiographical Writings, circa 1960s–circa

1970s), 4, Archives of American Art, Smithsonian Institution, https://www.aaa.si.edu/collections/alma-thomas-papers-9241.

"I've never bothered": Eleanor Munro, "The Late Springtime of Alma Thomas: Conversations with the Washington Colorist, from an Absorbing New Book," *Washington Post Magazine*, April 15, 1979.

"In my opinion, Black art": Alma Thomas papers, 7.

"Through color I have sought": Alma Thomas papers, 6.

24. Joan Mitchell

"the clouds and the sky": Mary Gabriel, *Ninth Street Women: Lee Krasner, Elaine De Kooning, Grace Hartigan, Joan Mitchell, and Helen Frankenthaler; Five Painters and the Movement That Changed Modern Art*. (New York: Back Bay Books, 2019), 358.

"rusty leaves": Joan Mitchell, "Autumn," *Poetry*, December 1935, 129.

"My paintings repeat a feeling": *Joan Mitchell: Portrait of an Abstract Painter*, directed by Marion Cajori (A Christian Blackwood Co-Production, Arthouse Films, 1992).

"When I was discouraged": Joan Mitchell, oral history interview by Linda Nochlin, April 16, 1986, transcript, Archives of American Art, Smithsonian Institution,

https://www.aaa.si.edu/collections/interviews/oral
-history-interview-joan-mitchell-12183#transcript.
"riding a bike with no hands": Phillip Barcio, "Vibrancy
and Energy in Joan Mitchell Paintings," *IdeelArt
Magazine*, October 30, 2016, https://www.ideelart
.com/magazine/joan-mitchell.
"She has led the kind": Bill Berkson, "Tiger, Tiger: A Few Days
with Joan," *Poetry*, February 2013, via Poetry Foundation,
https://www.poetryfoundation.org/poetrymagazine
/articles/69918/tiger-tiger-a-few-days-with-joan.

Index

Page numbers in **bold** refer to artwork and illustrations

INDEX

About the Authors

Jean Leibowitz is a portrait and landscape artist who uses traditional painting and drawing approaches in her art. She lives in Portland, Maine.

Lisa LaBanca Rogers is a former elementary school librarian and the award-winning author of *16 Words: William Carlos Williams and "The Red Wheelbarrow"* and *Hound Won't Go.* She regularly writes about art and artists for various magazines. She lives in Boston.